PAPIER MÂCHÉ PRINCESS

PAPIER MÂCHÉ PRINCESS

A Memoir of Breaking Free

MARIE ISOM

MEDIA.COM

Dedication

To Scott, my Silver Fox. You have always believed I could, so I did. You are the best part of my life.

To my children, Kyle, Josh, Alyssa, Matthew, Michelle, and Elizabeth: You are the most amazing humans, and I am so grateful for your presence in this world. You make it a better place, and you make me a better person. I love you more than you can fathom.

To my grandchildren, Mason, Theo, Caeris, and Ophie: You are the icing on the cake.

And in memory of Mr. LaClair: I carried your words and encouragement with me for decades, even if I wasn't always brave enough to take them out and look at them. You made such a difference in this world, and I hope that you can see from heaven how many souls you touched.

Contents

PART THREE:
ILLUSION OF CONTROL

PART FOUR:
LOOSENING MY GRIP

PART FIVE:
INTO ABUNDANCE

Acknowledgments

Writing this book was the scariest and hardest thing I have ever done, and it wouldn't exist without the constant love and support from my husband, Scott. You encourage me to go beyond what I think I am capable of. I love you forever.

My deepest gratitude goes to my prayer team: Becky Jones, Dawn Roberts, Amy Paris, Donna Brooks, Jen Combs, Jennifer Anderson-Tyrell, Marci Walters, Rachel Stovall, Shannon Tisher, and Nancy Garcia, with a humongous special thanks to prayer team coordinator, Donna Petrie. Donna, you have been a constant encourager and prayer warrior. Words can't adequately convey my love and appreciation.

Danny Brown, you have encouraged me to constantly look to the Lord for direction and strength . . . and to write. Thank you for being a godly spiritual mentor and friend.

Sheila Seifert, who first pushed me to move the words out of my private notebooks and into sharing them with others, thank you for your wisdom and encouragement.

To Susan Underwood and my classmates from Center for Christian Coaching who taught me how to break the overwhelming into do-able steps: Jan Edwards, Jennifer Coppinger, Jennifer Tyrell, Kim Miller, Maria Vargas, Melissa Judy, and Ollie McPherson.

And to master writing coach extraordinaire Karen Bouchard, you have been one of God's most amazing gifts. Thank you for never letting me quit.

I pray that the book itself is an acknowledgment that there is One who came to give life and give it abundantly: Jesus the Messiah. I am eternally grateful.

Introduction

June 2018

AS A GENTLE BREEZE ATONED FOR THE RELENTLESS HEAT, my husband
and I strolled, hand in hand, reading restaurant menus in the Lowry
Dining District of Denver. Café Mercato, Lucky Cat, North Country.
There were too many choices, and my stomach growled in protest of
our indecisiveness. I put my free hand above my eyes, squinting against
the blazing Colorado sunshine and practically salivated over Masterpiece
Kitchen's choices.

I turned to make a funny comment to Scott. At that moment, a black
Mercedes-Benz slowly rolled past, its windows down and music blaring.

My humorous comment evaporated.

I flinched, my mouth dried up, and my back tightened. I scanned the
area for a place to hide because out of nowhere an image of the passenger
pulling out a gun and shooting my husband and me point blank flashed
through my mind.

Gruesome, I know. But for many years, images like this have launched
surprise attacks. I am never really prepared for them. They ambush me
at the most random and unexpected moments. They pummel me until
I recognize them for what they are and pin them to the ground with

1

truth. I remind myself that these PTSD (post-traumatic stress disorder) moments have no real power over me.

Getting to this place of victory has come at a cost. Fear and anxiety didn't just bow down in defeat when I first challenged them. I couldn't just close my eyes, whisper three Scriptures, and click my heels to land in freedom. I had to step into the arena. And when I did, I lost a few rounds. Got some cuts and bruises. Got knocked down.

But each time I hit the mat, my faith shouted, "Get back up! PTSD moments might taunt you, but they do not win. They do not hold the scepter. Neither does the violent crime that instigated them."

The event that has haunted me occurred just after midnight on July 20, 2012. On that night, my two teenage daughters and I sat in a packed movie theater in Aurora, Colorado, watching the opening scenes of the newly released *The Dark Knight Rises*. Suddenly, a deranged gunman entered the room and showed me that evil isn't just some story on the evening news. Evil is something that can—and did—strut into my personal space and forever alter my world.

Twelve people died that night.

My daughters and I survived.

But that doesn't mean we weren't changed forever.

For years—long before that fateful night in the theater—I had fought desperately to be in control, battling myself, God, and others to gain it. And for a brief time, I thought I had won. As CEO of my life, I gripped my circumstances, my family, my health, and, most important, my image, tightly in my hand. Yet when I unclenched my fingers, I realized I had been holding nothing more than the wind.

The Aurora shooting made that abundantly clear.

My skewed relationship with control began back in my childhood when I faced countless traumatic moments and truly had *no* control. Many times as a child, I hid under blankets, trying to shut out the sounds of yelling and fighting that were taking place downstairs.

Uncertainty defined my youth, and I ignorantly declared that I would never allow myself to be vulnerable again. I would take control of my life. I would be free and do whatever I thought best for myself. Instead, I went from having *no* control as a child to *losing* control in my teenage years. Alcohol abuse, depression, and bulimia took a toll on my body, soul, and spirit.

Finally, weary and determined, I grabbed at control. As a young wife and mother, I resolved to serve God and learn and "do good," so I would finally be someone worthy. But convincing myself, under the guise of religion, that I was finally captain of my own ship was nothing more than an *illusion* of control.

Hanging on to an illusion is exhausting. Eventually the illusion shatters, revealing the truth.

I knew I needed a better way. I needed a life *out of control*—out of my control and into the trust of a good and loving God.

Ironically, in the process of letting go of my attempts to control life's outcomes, I have discovered the abundant life God designed me for, the life I have craved all along.

Of course, it is easy to shout the words "I'm letting go!" But is not always easy to walk the walk. When I was in my forties, I came across a quote by Madeleine L'Engle: "When we were children, we used to think that when we were grown up we would no longer be vulnerable. But to grow up is to be vulnerable . . . to be alive is to be vulnerable."

I'm still learning to let go and to live vulnerably. Though my victories have been hard-won at times, there is much prosperity, freedom, peace, and deep joy in the lessons.

For many years, people have encouraged me to write my story. I have also felt the prompting of the Holy Spirit to share what He has done in my life. But responding to that prompting has been one of the most challenging things I have ever done, particularly when it came to writing about childhood. I have resisted, mostly because none of us live our lives in isolation. My childhood story involves other people. They are people I love dearly and have come to understand better since growing up, and more important, since God replaced my heart of stone with a new, Spirit-filled heart.

As I've penned these words, there is no condemnation or judgment in my heart toward others in my story. I am intimately acquainted with personal failures and bad choices. Like Paul the apostle, I could surely declare, "I am chief of sinners."

My aim is to share my story of how God took a broken, shame-filled girl, desperate to control her life and her image, and graciously set her free.

Most important, I have tried to find a place of truth and grace, which are powerful when they are weaved together, as God intended.

The psalmist wrote: "Graciousness and [a]truth have met together; righteousness and peace have kissed each other." (Psalm 85:10 NASB).

The beauty of truth and grace was really brought home to me last summer when my husband and I were visiting Chapin Orchards, in Essex Junction, Vermont. While we paid for heavy-duty sacks to carry the fruit we would pick, the chatty cashier directed us to the correct area of the orchard. Rows of short trees dotted with red apples beckoned us. Before we headed over to them, the proprietor gave us very clear picking instructions. "Only the Macintosh are ready. You can tell the Macintosh trees because they have the orange cones in front of them." She pointed off into the distance. "The rest are off limits. They won't be ripe for weeks. Remember, only Macintosh," she repeated. That was fine with me. Macintosh are my favorite apple.

Scott and I made our way across the slightly damp ground. Though there was a nip in the air, the clouds had scattered, and bright blue skies cheered us on. I was so engrossed in our conversation that I barely noticed what I was pulling from the trees. It didn't take long to fill our bags, but we continued walking down the rows, chatting nonstop. When we got to the end of a row of trees that looked like short, plump sentinels, we turned and walked back towards the barn.

I took one of the apples from my bag and bit into it. *Not as good as I expected,* I thought. Still, I munched absentmindedly while we walked and chatted. Then an unfamiliar voice interrupted our conversation. "Are you eating a Red Delicious?" a man asked.

I looked up and saw a man—another proprietor I assumed—striding towards us.

"Uh no, we picked Macintosh," I responded.

"Nope, that's a Red Delicious," he stated matter-of-factly.

I started to protest, certain we had picked from the trees with the orange cones. The man pulled off his baseball cap, swiped at his brow, and placed the cap back on his head.

"Here, let me show you." He took one of the apples from my bag and flipped it upside down. He indicated that I do the same with the one in my hand. The difference was immediately apparent. The Macintosh had a round, smooth bottom while the one I held had four distinct quadrants. A Red Delicious. I felt my face turning pink, and I shrugged sheepishly. "Sorry."

The fellow pointed into my bag. "I think you have a couple more of the Red Delicious in there."

Sure enough, I pulled out two more of the off-limit apples and handed them to the proprietor. He walked over and tossed them under a tree. I apologized again.

"I'm actually relieved, though," I confessed with a chuckle. "Because that was the worst Mackintosh apple I have ever eaten."

The fellow laughed and waved off our apology. "It happens all the time, and it is nothing compared to some of the things I've seen. One of these days I'm going to write a book about a few of the characters who have visited our orchard."

He then went on to explain why he took the time to stop us and point out my error. "You know, you could have left our orchard and given us bad reviews, telling people that the apples here are really lousy, when in fact, you were eating unripe apples of an entirely different type than you thought."

"I guess my chapter in your book can be called the "Apple of Shame" or "Eating Forbidden Fruit," I joked.

He laughed and told us to go ahead and add a few more apples to our bag. He showed us the correct way to twist and pull an apple from the tree, then walked away with a smile and a wave.

Back in our hotel that night, I brushed minty toothpaste across my teeth and mused on the grace the orchard man had shown us. He didn't let me get away with believing I was eating a Macintosh or picking the wrong apples. But he didn't make fun of me. He didn't condemn me. He didn't yell at me. And he certainly didn't shame me.

Instead, he educated, encouraged, and humored us while he spoke truth about the apple I was eating. His gentle correction reminded me of the way God gently admonishes and teaches—with grace and truth. And it reminded me that when we carry a palette of compassion and mercy with us, we can face truth head-on—both past and present—without the need to paint pastoral postcards of pretense. Beauty and healing naturally emerge with each brush stroke of grace.

Like the proprietor at the apple orchard, and like the psalmist in the Scriptures, that is how I seek to view the stories of people I encounter in my life, how I have written my story.

It is also how I hope and pray that you receive the words in this book.

As truth intertwined with grace.

PART ONE: NO CONTROL

Despair (1978)

Little Girl, why do you weep?
The sun will rise again.
And who tells you lies, Old Woman?

1: The Roots of Chaos

Early 1970s

"Lily is here!"

My sister's shout momentarily froze me. I grabbed my half-dressed Barbie, bolted for the stairs, and threw myself on the double bed that I shared with my older sister. I yanked the light blue bedspread over my head. The yarn fringe from its border caught in my fingers, and I fought to get them free.

Beneath the bedspread, I squeezed my eyes shut, but it didn't matter. The darkness couldn't protect me from the sounds of shouting and expletives assaulting me from the first floor. My stomach hurt.

"Please go away. Please go away. Please go away," I whispered over and over. I pleaded for the woman downstairs, the one I knew owned a gun, to go away and leave my mom and my family alone.

A short time later—minutes? Half an hour?—the shouts ended. I tentatively raised my head from under the blanket. Confusion cut through the fear. Why was my shirt wet, as though a cup of water had spattered all over me? Wet circles spread under my arms too. It was wintertime. I didn't understand why I was sweating.

I was eight. I had no idea fear releases chemicals that turn sweat glands into faucets. The weird dampness was just a random puzzle piece around the periphery of the moment, and the questions evaporated faster than the perspiration.

Her name was Lily.

The name suggested a lovely flower, as though she added beauty and joy to her surroundings. Nothing could have been further from the truth.

I called her Crazy Lily. Poison Ivy or Cactus would have been fitting names as well. She was the ex-wife of one of Mom's friends, and even the shadow of her presence frightened me.

When her white station wagon pulled up in front of our duplex, it sent shivers down my spine. The sight of her marching towards our front door like a school bully crossing the playground sometimes paralyzed me. Other times it sent me running for cover beneath my bedspread.

My mom and dad were still married at the time, but the marriage was falling apart. My mom had been spending time with Lily's ex-husband. It was clear that Lily was not happy about it. Sometimes she merely yelled and cussed at my mother.

Other times I could hear glass shattering, and even behind my clenched eyes I could envision a Pepsi bottle being thrown across the room, its brown liquid staining wallpaper and coloring my sense of safety a shade of sticky, black mess. Sometimes Crazy Lily went beyond verbal attacks, and on more than one occasion she waved a gun around while shouting threats. She never used it, but it still terrified me.

Later in life I would look back and realize fear brought on by traumatic events is often the seed to a slew of other imprisoning emotions. Children do not have the ability to understand and process all the complexities of adult relationships and behaviors. Today, I'm able to wipe the steam from the mirror, and see things differently. But during those early years, the tiniest kernels of fear-induced anger fell into empty places, holes where childlike trust and innocence had been unintentionally yanked out. These seeds of those events would be watered and fed over the following years, eventually reaping a massive harvest of cynicism, shame, depression, hatred, self-loathing, and jealousy.

Fear became a demanding boss, controlling my beliefs and actions.

There were good moments during those early years. I loved elementary school, learning multiplication tables, and penmanship. I thrived on knowing what to expect in the classroom, and I had friends in the neighborhood. After the yellow school bus dropped us off at the end of each school day, I freely roamed the streets with my siblings and other neighborhood children. We played kick the can, hide 'n' seek, freeze tag, and other games.

My friend Becky lived across the street, and the real world where our parents drank and got into loud, ugly fights faded into the shadows when the two of us pulled out our Barbie and Ken dolls with their endless wardrobe choices. We got to control the story, and it always had a happily-ever-after ending. Only the jingle of the ice cream truck pulled us from our make-believe realm long enough to stand in line, trying to choose between an orange sherbet Push-up Pop or Strawberry Shortcake ice cream bar.

Yes, there were fun childhood moments with Barbies, sherbet, freeze tag, and even trips to Santa's Village. Like antique polaroid photos, these happy images faded through my teenage and early adult years and became harder to make out. They became buried beneath large, weighty albums filled with pictures of empty whiskey bottles, overflowing ashtrays, and our chipped Formica table covered with dirty plates of dried food when I woke up. These photo albums of my soul bring back memories of sleepless nights when the noise of partying and fighting lasted until the early morning hours.

As my early elementary years progressed, my parents' marriage began to crumble. Or maybe as I got older, I just became more aware of the adult tension, the days fraught with anger and blame or thick silence and the nights spent drinking. Either way, I never knew what to expect. The unpredictability of their day-to-day relationship created a constant uneasiness and sense of dread in my young mind.

My mother was petite, dark-haired, and beautiful. Her twinkling brown eyes could light up a room, and I loved her fiercely, loved her cooking and loved the way she could make our home look pretty and inviting.

Some afternoons I would run home from the bus stop, burst through the front door, and discover a plate of whoopie pies sitting on the counter, the sweet, cream-filled cakes a testimony to my mother's cooking skills.

On days like that, at the sight of her sitting quietly in a rocking chair, a paperback in one hand and a Winston cigarette in the other, I would let out the breath I didn't know I was holding.

Sometimes at 5 o'clock my dad would walk in the door, remove his tie and jacket, and we would all sit around the dinner table devouring my mom's fried chicken and creamy mashed potatoes or beef stew and buttery rolls. But those days became less and less the norm.

At first, the whiskey and beer flowed only on weekends, accompanied by a constant influx of people I didn't know, and my sense of security was replaced with a continual worry and niggling anxiety. Soon the drunken laughter and coarse joking invaded our weekdays as well.

One incident among many stands out.

"Hey, I wanted those!" I complained to my older brother, Phil, who grinned as he poured the last of the Boo Berries into his bowl. I scowled and reached for the Fruity Pebbles. I hated the colorful rice cereal because it took all of five seconds before they turned into a soggy mess. I wanted the little marshmallows that dissolved in my mouth. I frowned at my brother and struggled with the milk container. A strange sound startled me, and I sloshed milk onto the table. The sound was coming from the living room. I got up to investigate.

Sprawled across the couch was a dark-haired, shirtless man. His pants were wet. In the crotch. Eww! I had no idea who he was. Genesee beer bottles lay on the floor next to him. There was a stench in the room, one I would come to recognize as a mixture of perspiration, urine, and beer. Some hybrid of a snore and snort escaped his open mouth. I backed into the kitchen, turned around, and grabbed the Fruity Pebbles box. I shook the cereal around and dug my hand in, searching for the prize.

I hoped it was a magic ring that could transport me someplace different. Someplace away from strange drunk men who partied with my parents all night and could be found passed out on our sofa in the morning.

During those years, a skewed picture of marriage and men began to form in my young mind. My parents' relationship became more volatile. Neither of my parents ever physically harmed us. But their loud fights—the screaming and cursing —created a rock in the pit of my stomach.

Their fights sometimes went beyond angry words.

They occasionally shattered dishes, punched walls and tables, and once knocked over a Christmas tree. One night my father had his hands around my mother's neck, choking her, until the sounds of me and my siblings sobbing and screaming at him to stop broke through his drunkenness. He let go and stormed out of the house.

One of the many things my parents fought about was my father's infidelity. He was handsome, and I would later learn he had always been a ladies' man. Though the names changed, he usually had girlfriends on the side, and sometimes they had the audacity to call my mother and complain about his cheating ways.

One day, my brother ran home from the bus stop faster than usual, his grin bigger than the whoopie pie he was about to shove in his mouth.

"I have a girlfriend!" he exclaimed, spitting bits of chocolate cake as he made his big announcement.

My mom continued rinsing a Tupperware mixing bowl and beaters. "That's nice."

"Yeah, her name is Allison, and she's so pretty!"

Mom turned from the faucets and wiped her hands on an embroidered dish towel. "Allison who?"

"Allison Ferguson! She has blonde hair, and she likes me." Phil couldn't stop grinning.

"She can't be your girlfriend." The sharpness in my mother's voice startled us.

"Why not?" Phil asked.

"Because she is your half-sister."

Not long after that, I spent the night at my friend Karen's house. Before settling in for the night, we rummaged through her mom's jewelry box, trying on long necklaces and bracelets.

"Ooh, what a pretty locket!" I reached for the engraved oval dangling from a sturdy chain and struggled to unclasp it.

"That's my mom's boyfriend," Karen giggled at the photo inside.

I looked closer. "Hey, it looks like my dad!"

We laughed at the coincidence, put the jewelry away, and headed off to brush our teeth and get ready for bed. I had brought my new yellow pajamas. They had ruffled bloomer bottoms and a sleeveless top with lace around the collar. I quickly forget about the locket.

The next morning, Karen and I raced to the kitchen for strawberry pop tarts. I hoped they were the kind with icing. My excitement turned to confusion when I saw my father putting on his jacket. He glanced at me without a word and then headed out the door.

We never talked about that night.

Craving something I couldn't have put into words, I created a fantasy, a nighttime movie reel to lull myself to sleep during the late nights of drinking and fighting that took place more and more often. In the repeating scene that I played in my head each night, my child-hood crush—a blonde-haired, blue-eyed boy named Randy—and I lived together in a tiny cottage by a river. The serenading of the slow-moving water in my fantasy world calmed my spirit. Randy and I held hands, strolling by the water, without a care in the world. Safe. Serene. Quiet. I later dubbed this my River Story.

Night after night, I conjured up these images to paint over the reality of constant chaos and confusion in my home, but it was a futile attempt.

I didn't have the power to create order, and I certainly could not bring stability to the relationships of the adults in my life.

Colorful glass rectangles formed a border around the top of a tiny square room that served as an entryway to our duplex. They reminded me of the stained-glass images in the Catholic church we sometimes visited. Once, after a particularly volatile weekend, my dad stood in that box-like room with a suitcase in each hand. A decade of married life had been reduced to a few folded shirts, slacks, and striped ties.

An argument between my parents the night before had been ferocious, and my father was moving out. Again. Now, the setting sunlight shoved through the colored glass and created ever-changing shadows on his tired face. He set the suitcases down. Suddenly he clutched his chest. "My heart. My heart," he gasped. My mom immediately crushed out her cigarette in an overflowing ashtray and ran to him, fear momentarily overriding the sorrow that had aged her.

Within minutes, my father was lying down on the sofa in the living room. My mom was anxiously unbuttoning his shirt and tending to him. In the past, I'd heard the grown-ups murmur about heart issues, about heart attacks that had taken the men in his family at young ages. Whether my father had a real attack or if it was a ploy, I never knew. But once again, the official splitting of my parents' marriage didn't happen. My dad remained in the house, and my mom's new boyfriend, Gerald, was not happy.

I adored Gerald, imagining he was my mother's knight in shining armor who would rescue us from the chaos and uncertainty of daily life. I craved stability more than I craved orange cream Push-Ups or cookie-coated Strawberry Shortcake bars from the ice cream truck. I thought with Gerald we would have it at last. Even then I was beginning to understand that stability gives a sense of being in control. It feels safe, and it seemed to me that my mom's boyfriend carried the promise of safety into our lives as easily as he carried his usual six pack of Pabst Blue Ribbon.

Sometimes Gerald and I conspired together after my mom had passed out from a night of partying. We'd collect the remaining liquor bottles in the house and dump what was left into the kitchen sink. I felt special and connected—and in control—as we watched the smelly liquid swirl down the drain, working together to rescue my mom from her drinking.

Gerald lived in a trailer down a dirt road surrounded by verdant acres of land. Sometimes my mom and we five kids spent the day, or the weekend, at his trailer. Those were some of my best childhood days.

On the way there, to his trailer, my sisters and I would stand in the back of Gerald's green pickup truck, belting out the lyrics of the popular Bo Donaldson and the Heywood's song or "Delta Dawn" or some other country hit of the day. "Like a rhinestone cowboy," we'd sing at the top of our lungs as I pulled wisps of hair from my mouth and the dust rose like applause behind us.

I hoped my mom would marry this man so that we could move in with him. Despite being unkempt, Gerald's trailer was one of my favorite places to be. Peace filled me when I strolled down the dirt road and daydreamed about my mother marrying him. In the tales I mentally spun, she was no longer enslaved to alcohol. Instead, my sober mom would clean the messy trailer and use her decorating talents to transform the inside to a place as beautiful and serene as the surrounding landscape.

I imagined her adding colorful curtains, vases of plastic flowers, and other knick-knacks. It would be a forever home rather than a place we occasionally visited, a place where my siblings and I picked blackberries and fed crab apples to baby pigs in a pen and made ourselves dizzy on a tire swing hanging from an umbrella shaped tree in front of the old mobile home.

But mom and Gerald's relationship teeter-tottered like my parents' marriage.

A few nights after the heart episode that kept my father from moving out, Gerald and Mom got into a huge fight. Gerald towered over Mom's tiny frame.

"He's a @!# , and you are a stupid #@!& for staying with him. You need to make up your @!# mind!"

Every scream, every cuss word, every slamming of his fist on the table caused me to shrivel up inside of myself. Soon I began to see a side to Gerald that I despised, a side that fed my young belief that adults could not be trusted.

During one of their arguments, when their screams reached the ceiling and boomeranged fear back down on me, Gerald suddenly raised his leg and kicked our fish tank. The glass shattered and the water gushed out, forming a large puddle.

Something inside of me broke and spilled as well. My new hopes and dreams for a more peaceful life floundered alongside the goldfish in the puddle on the floor of our Lincoln Avenue home. Nothing was ever going to change. Gerald was no knight in shining armor. He was no different than the rest of the adults.

My mother's relationship with Gerald only grew more explosive and my father's presence in our home didn't help.

I remember one night when my parents and a bunch of their friends sat around drinking at our house. My siblings and I were up way past our bedtime, but no one seemed to notice. Soon the bickering around the kitchen table turned to arguing. At one point, my father mumbled that he was going to shoot himself. He took his pistol from the gun cabinet and stumbled outside.

Boom!

The shot jolted me, my siblings, and everyone else in the house. Silence followed. No one knew what to do. The adults sat frozen as we kids cried and hugged each other. Finally, my father sauntered back into the house and declared to the sobered-up group at the table, "None of you care if I live or die." Then he laughed.

I felt sick. The fear, confusion, and anger of that moment twisted themselves together into a thick cord that squeezed what little hope I had left.

Turbulent, incomprehensible moments like these were shaping my heart, my brain chemistry, and my beliefs about who I was. The shape was becoming uglier and more distorted as the days passed.

Another night, sometime around the beginning of my fourth-grade year, my mother had gone out to bars with her friends and came home with a black eye. I never learned how she got it, but the next morning, a hangover kept her in bed. She was supposed to be babysitting a little boy that day, as she regularly did. I stayed home from school, and she gave me instructions through her closed bedroom door.

"When Stevie's mom gets here, tell her I ran to the store for a minute and that you'll watch him until I return." When the woman and child arrived, I delivered the line just like I was supposed to do. But Stevie's mom did not leave.

"I'll just wait," the woman said with an odd smile before she settled herself on our sofa.

I didn't know what to do. An awkward silence ensued.

"Um, I have to go to the bathroom," I finally said, unable to look her in the eye. I raced upstairs, pounded on my mother's bedroom door, and loudly whispered that Stevie's mom wasn't leaving.

When my mom didn't respond, I opened the door and was shocked to see a strange man with her. I yanked the door closed, then slowly walked down the stairs and tried to be as nonchalant as my stunned nine-year-old self knew how to be.

In ten minutes or so, my mother came down the stairs in her bathrobe. Her black-eye and stale whiskey breath added to an already rough appearance. Keeping my eyes on the floor, the ceiling, anywhere but Stevie's mom, I mumbled to the boy's mother, "Uh, she must have come back home without me seeing her."

We both knew I was lying. The woman's pity toward me was palpable, and a deep shame fell on my soul, like a coating of tar. Hot, heavy, suffocating tar. That sense of defectiveness would cling to me for years. And it would be reinforced time and time again throughout my adolescence. Whenever these kinds of events happened, and it was often, I told myself they were no big deal. I'd read stories about kids whose parents beat them, belittled them, or locked them in attics. My parents weren't like that. I can't recall a single spanking, though I know there were threats of them. I knew my parents would never intentionally harm me.

But damage isn't always done by the magnitude of an earthquake. A slow leak can cause just as much damage to a foundation. All the persistent, seemingly minor incidents add up and can be just as destructive. I would spend the next several decades trying to duct-tape my own brokenness into something solid to stand on.

Trying to fix each crack.

Trying to create a picture of wholeness.

Trying to control the image.

But all my efforts were in vain. At the end of the day, I was just a taped together mess.

2: Divorce

MY FIRST FEELINGS OF DEEP HAPPINESS BEGAN, oddly enough, with my parents' divorce. I didn't anticipate the strange mix of relief and optimism that welled up in me when my mother and father finally announced their impending divorce. This new feeling grew for several months. It seemed odd to have felt such a thing as hope at the splintering of my family. Yet the uncertainty, the late nights of drinking, and the fighting between my mother and father and others—along with my growing anxieties—had created a cloud of dysphoria that followed me wherever I went.

My mother had kicked my father out before, but for various reasons—like chest pains—it never lasted. *This* time, when my parents announced they were divorcing, it was different. This time it was really happening. I had hope. I expected life would become calmer, more stable, and more predictable.

In some respects, the season after the divorce met my young expectations. With help from friends, my mother packed her meager belongings, along with us five kids' clothing and toys. I traded Barbie outfits with Becky, my friend from across the street, one last time, and I cried as I said goodbye to her. I felt some apprehension about the unknown when my family waved a final farewell to the duplex on Lincoln Avenue. But mostly I felt hope reignite as we headed to the tiny town of Bakersfield, Vermont.

The quaint town boasted an area of about forty-five square miles with a population of around seven hundred.

Though barely a blip on any map, Bakersfield stole my heart. The first thing I fell in love with was our little rental house. It was near the edge of town and sat on a sprawling shag rug of soft green grass interwoven with buttercups. A tiny trickling brook and miniature footbridge graced the yard, and for a moment I thought parts of my River Story fantasy had come to life.

I was about to get my first taste of the carefree childhood I had always longed for.

In the new house, I again shared a bedroom with my younger and older sisters, but our new room was huge. Sunshine poured in through the windows. We had a walk-in closet with shelves, which excited me—I couldn't wait to organize my Barbies and books and clothing.

On the first day of my new elementary school, I pushed my cereal bowl away after one spoonful of peanut butter Cap'n Crunch cereal. Nervousness attached itself to my excitement, and I couldn't eat. I grabbed my sweater and walked slowly to the edge of the road in front of our house to wait for the bus with my brother and sisters.

Questions growled louder than my empty stomach. *Would I make friends? What would the teachers be like? Would I get good grades like I did in St. Albans?* School had always been a safe environment, and I hoped it would be the same in our new town.

My worries quickly disappeared. During that very first week of fourth grade at Bakersfield Elementary school, Molly, one of the prettiest girls I had ever seen, passed a note to me. "Will you be my best friend? Yes or No." I circled yes, and just like that, I belonged.

It was a season of freedom and friendships, maple creemees at the little corner market, and school magazine sales with prizes of long, fat pretzel sticks and fuzzy, googly-eyed stickers. It was a time of flavored roll-on lip gloss, sleepovers with new girlfriends, and my first kiss from a boy named Hazen.

My mom still left us at home while she went out partying, but it didn't matter. Not even waking to the smell of stale cigarettes and booze or strangers in the house bothered me. Life was good. That spring was magical and nothing could mar it.

But the magic was fleeting.

Just months after my mom rented the lovely little house with the brook, the first place that finally felt like home, Dave, one of the men who had helped her move, decided to buy the house, forcing us to move.

Dave Hescott. His name became synonymous with traitor in my young mind. I hated him the way juveniles hate when they can't see beyond their own personal world. I blamed him for ruining everything. Leaving that house was so hard.

I left behind pieces of my heart, the fragile bits of hope that I had collected in that tiny Vermont town. That summer—the summer between fourth and fifth grade, when Double-Crossing Dave and his family took over the house we had rented—my mother and her five children became homeless. Not living-on-the-streets homeless, but no-place-to-call-home homeless.

For a time, we stayed with some of my mom's friends. We shared their rundown trailer which sat on a huge plot of land somewhere near Montgomery, Vermont. I remember we played in an ice-cold creek during the day and chased fireflies at night. I also remember how much I didn't want to be there, and my sadness dressed itself in sullenness and anger.

The drinking among the adults seemed to rise with the summer humidity and temperatures. I hated my mother's drunk friends. I hated the trailer. I hated my life. I hated having no control over where we lived or who we were with. I hated being forced to hang out with the children of my mom's friends. And the weight of shame still clung to me, hot and heavy as the humidity.

One night I sat outside the trailer and slapped at the mosquitos on my arms and legs. Staring into the flickering flames of a little campfire,

I felt annoyed at the kids chasing each other around me. The laughter of my mother and her friends supplied off-tune back-up vocals to Tammy Wynette's hit *D-I-V-O-R-C-E* that made its way outside from an old record player inside the crowded mobile home.

Suddenly screams and cries rose above the music, and I looked in horror at the flames in my three-year-old brother's hair. One of the kids had tossed a soda can into the fire, totally unaware it was filled with gas. The can exploded, and my brother was on fire. His shoulders were severely burned, leaving scars that decades later finally faded to a dull pink. The blame landed on the children of my mother's friends, and their father whipped them with a thin switch until their cries turned to whimpers and snot ran down their faces.

It was a long time before I could forget the sound of their cries, a long time before I could get the smell of burnt hair and burnt flesh out of my nostrils. And it was much longer before I let go of my anger at the adults that I blamed more than the children.

Shortly after that, my two sisters and I were sent back to Bakersfield to live with one of my mother's older sisters and her husband. Aunt Pauline and Uncle Don were gracious and loving. They had a large home, and they welcomed us with open arms. Although they had six children of their own, some of them had grown and moved out, leaving empty, furnished rooms behind.

I should be thrilled to be in a stable environment, in the town I love, I thought as I sat on the double bed with its white quilt. The room had ruffled curtains and matching furniture. It was the nicest room I had ever slept in. But despite the beautiful furnishings and the people with big hearts who had taken us in, there was no comfort for me there. Comfort is so often tied to familiarity, and there was nothing familiar about my new setting. Living with my cousins felt weird in more ways than just the décor.

Aunt Pauline and Uncle Don were teetotalers and devout Catholics. We kids had chores: sometimes sitting on the porch and removing peas from their pods and other times doing yard work. We also had routines: set mealtimes and bedtimes. Perhaps if my stay there had lasted longer, I would have grown accustomed to this new kind of life and the stability I craved. Instead, I felt out of place.

The day my mom showed up and announced she had found a place to rent, I clapped my hands and grinned from ear to ear. We would all be together again. I expected another Bakersfield-esque move, and I was thrilled.

Until we moved into the apartment at 2 Province Street, Richford, Vermont.

The huge, dilapidated apartment building was clothed in olive-green paint faded by harsh Vermont weather. It sagged on the corner of Province Street and Eastern Avenue, much like a hunched-over beggar in an old military jacket. It housed five or six apartments. A long, skinny porch led to the space I would call home for the next few years.

The six of us squeezed into the new rental. The kitchen, dining room, and living room offered about five hundred square feet of living space. It had yellowed linoleum, outdated appliances, peeling wallpaper, and a smell like hard-boiled eggs wrapped in dirty laundry that haunted the small space. A tiny room attached to the kitchen became my mom's bedroom. Narrow stairs led into a small open space next to two bedrooms with stained, torn wallpaper.

My hopes sagged like the apartment. This place was nothing like our Bakersfield home. But at least the apartment meant my sisters and I were reunited with my mother and two brothers, and I was back on some familiar turf. As unstable as that ground may have been, it was what I knew.

In our new apartment, Elvis, Johnny Cash, Tammy Wynette, and other country music legends once again reigned, and I sang along with the well-known lyrics that poured from mom's tired, old record player. Even today, a Patsy Cline song can link arms with my current life and escort me back to that era, back to the way my bare legs stuck to the faux leather sleeper couch, back to the cigarette smoke that rose above our chipped Formica table and danced a drunken waltz with the unsightly fly traps spiraling down from the ceiling.

I sang, but the songs were not a strong enough antidote to defeat the anger, the sadness, and confusion welling up inside of me. My mom had a boyfriend who began speaking to me in a perverted way, explaining what boys would do to me, laughing and telling me that I better hope my childlike figure would develop so I could please the boys. "You're flatter than a board that's never been nailed," he said, taunting me. He also used vulgar words.

The hatred that began over the summer festered and grew, along with the sadness and anger and confusion.

I hated his graphic, filthy words.

I hated his presence in our lives.

I hated him.

His words watered my own self-hatred. I despised my body, my appearance, my very being. I felt as filthy as his talk. These emotions became a part of me; they stuck fast and ugly like those dead flies on the sticky brown strips dangling over my head. I unwittingly accepted them, the way children accept things, and they continued to shape me into a shame-filled adolescent, then later a cynical, seething, cupboard-door-slamming teenager, and eventually a young drunk.

During that first summer that we lived on Province Street, my siblings and I regularly collected all our empty beer and Pepsi bottles and lugged them to the little grocery store across the street. We exchanged the five and ten cent bottle refunds for Sugar Babies, Bottle Caps, and Marathon bars. I craved the sweets, but it didn't matter if I devoured the Sugar Babies in a single mouthful or forced myself to separate the Bottle Caps by color and savor them one at a time. I always wanted more.

Even when I saved the root beer flavored candy caps for last, they never filled the hunger in me. There was a craving I couldn't define, a hole much larger than the ones in the Marathon bar. I just didn't know that the longing had nothing to do with half-melted chocolate bars that left my fingers sticky and my heart still starving.

Although carting recyclable bottles to the store was a drag, it was much better than paying with food stamps. The government assistance money booklets added another layer of shame. When paying for my purchases with these tangible reminders of my family's poverty, I waited until other customers were busy elsewhere in the store. Then I would hurry to the counter and shove my items and food stamps towards the cashier. Small-town folks know each other, so I'm not sure what I thought I was hiding. I'd tap my feet impatiently while silently wishing for the small talk to end, so I could grab my change without anyone else seeing. I wanted to be done before the jangle of the door announced another presence.

Back in the 70s and 80s, food stamps came in booklets of varying colors depending on the value, and I was sure they shouted "Welfare!" to the world.

Synonymous with less than, I thought.

When the clerk handed me change, anything less than a dollar came in actual currency of nickels, dimes, and quarters. Sometimes my mom wanted to collect enough quarters to buy cigarettes or alcohol, neither of which you could buy with food stamps. She would send us kids over to the store with a paper dollar and instruct us to each buy a 25-cent piece of candy. If my siblings weren't around, I would have to do it a couple of times in a row. I wished I could slip on one of those plastic Halloween masks with the elastic strings to hide my identity, to cover my downcast eyes and pink cheeks. I hated being a welfare kid.

And I especially hated when my mom handed me a booklet of food stamps before she headed out of town.

"Here's five dollars." Mom's words had the slightest slur, the accent of Canadian Club whiskey only detectable by those with practice and experience. I had both, and I knew what was coming next. My heart sank.

"I'm going out with Noel."

She was leaving us for the night, and my siblings and I would use the food stamps to buy rotisserie chicken or grinders and potato chips until she returned.

Our apartment in Richford was a stone's throw from the Canadian border, and on many weekends my mother and her friends Cathy and Hazel would cross the border to spend the night drinking in Quebec. Sometimes my mom went with a new boyfriend instead of her girlfriends. Like tonight. Her new boyfriend was a Canadian, and I knew she wouldn't be back until at least tomorrow.

I devoured my turkey and cheese grinder. Licking potato chip crumbs from my fingers, I braced myself for another sleepless night.

Sleep always eluded me on the nights she was gone, because I was irrationally terrified of the mice that I could hear chewing and scratching in the wall of my bedroom. Sometimes I would go to the living room couch, but then I would hear the neighbor's rantings in the apartment below. We called him Crazy George. He had recently been released from a state mental hospital and many nights his incoherent grunts and jabbering would escape his apartment and find their way into ours. Sometimes the mutterings turned into shouts and banging. I was afraid of something more than the sound of his mutterings and shouts. My mother, who had a generous heart, often shared her record albums with George. I was afraid he would come to the door asking for one when she was gone.

During this season, the protective love I felt for my mother became overshadowed by my growing anger. I wanted her home. I wanted her to stop drinking. I wanted her to be healthy.

I wanted her to answer the door if George knocked.

When I was older, I came face to face with my own addictions. I could then look back with compassionate love and adult-sized understanding.

These, combined with the new life God breathed into my heart, evaporated every trace of the anger. But as a child, I foolishly and selfishly tried to control my mother. My ineffective tools consisted mostly of a sullen attitude, slamming doors, and dagger looks.

It wasn't long before I didn't have to worry about George anymore. One afternoon, I came home from school and discovered blood stains in front of his apartment. Mom told us George had tried to take his life and once again was in a mental hospital. Gaping at the marks he left behind, I wondered about what made him want to die. I wondered if I would ever have the desire to end my own life. If I ever got to that point, I hoped I didn't leave blood stains in front of a run-down apartment for townsfolk to gawk at.

Although George in the apartment downstairs made me nervous, the apartment building—and the town—had its share of nice people too.

Lisa, the younger sister of the woman renting the apartment closest to ours, introduced my siblings and me to other young people, including a few of her brothers. Once again, I played games like hide 'n' seek and kick-the-can with new friends. We tossed rocks into the Missisquoi River, which ran through town, rode bikes to the park, and I cautiously began to accept my new surroundings.

On the first day of fifth grade, I met a new friend while waiting at the bus stop. Sonya, a girl my age, lived just down the street. After shyly introducing ourselves, we sat together on the bus. It was a long ride to the edge of town where the elementary school sat back on a large plot of land framed by trees. I stared at the gorgeous setting. Sonya didn't seem to notice and chattered away as though we'd always been friends. I pulled my eyes from the window so I could listen to her and began to think I might like Richford after all.

On the ride back home after that first day of school, Sonya and I agreed to wear similar dresses and shoes the next day, sealing our friendship. I dreamed about belonging, about being accepted. I desperately wanted to be liked.

At my new school, fifth and sixth grades were combined. This meant I was in class with some of the older, most popular girls. They were pretty, athletic, and already beginning to develop shapely figures. I, on the other hand, could have been mistaken for a third grader. And a clumsy third grader at that. I constantly heard the words of my mother's boyfriend, even when I was alone. "You have a chest that is flatter than a board that has never been nailed, the boys won't like that."

I loathed my body even more. I wasn't just physically below average; his mocking words stunted my emotional growth. Jealousy of other girls festered within me. Once, I stuffed my training bra with tissues in an attempt to look like they did. My mom caught me and yelled at me, which put an end to the pretense but not the longing to be different than I was.

Despite my physical and emotional immaturity, one of the boys at my new school liked me, probably because I was a new fish in a stagnant pond. This didn't go over well with the older girls who were used to getting all the attention from the opposite sex.

One afternoon during gym class, I headed out with my classmates to a field to play a game of kickball. During the game, a couple of the older girls laughed and hooted when I dropped an easy catch, mocked the way I ran, and called me names when the teacher wasn't around. When gym class was over, sweaty students gathered the bases, and someone scooped up the red kickball before everyone sauntered in groups back to the school building. I lagged a little behind, hoping to avoid the three older girls. But instead of going on ahead, they waited for me.

"Dean only likes you because you are new here," one of them said. Another one tripped me, and when I fell, all three kicked me in the side before hurrying on ahead. "Actually, Marie, nobody likes you!" One of them called back to me. The others laughed and shouted their agreement.

The kicks didn't hurt as much as the laughter.

I picked myself up and tried not to cry, knowing that tears would only fuel more laughter. I trudged back to the classroom and avoided looking at anyone.

The physical bruises on my side were gone within a few days, and the incident was forgotten by the girls. It really was a minor thing, I told myself. But the truth was it had reopened emotional wounds that had not yet healed, and beliefs in my defectiveness bled out.

Those three girls and I would become on-again, off-again friends, playing jacks and spin-the-bottle with other kids, sleeping over at each others' houses, and passing notes back and forth at school.

But my soul remained skittish, never quite trusting people who befriended me.

3: Papier Mâché Princess

WHEN I WAS IN SIXTH GRADE AND FINALLY GETTING USED TO MY NEW NORMAL, my mom announced she was pregnant. Today, being unmarried and pregnant isn't considered a big deal. It was different then, and some of the girls made fun of me because of it. They reminded me that my mother wasn't like the other mothers.

All of this reinforced my beliefs that I would never measure up.

One day, my classmate Linda, who had long blonde hair and even longer legs, sent me a mocking note: *Your mom is a slut and so are you.*

I stared at the familiar handwriting then crumpled up the notebook paper and tossed it in the trash can. A few days later, Linda had forgotten about the note and chose me as her partner when we paired up to make topical maps. But her words wouldn't stay crumpled up and forgotten by me, not even after the garbage can was emptied. They were etched into my mind and stayed with me throughout junior high. They remained a background presence in high school.

Early on, I laughed, read, and did my best to be a top student. I played tetherball on the playground, sat with others at lunchtime, and phoned girlfriends in the evening to plan the next day's outfits. I had crushes on boys and looked forward to Fridays when we had fun classes like downhill skiing and pottery. I smiled and pretended I was like everyone else.

But I couldn't conquer the visceral belief that I was a nobody. Less than a nobody.

As a child, I once read a story about a piñata, a papier mâché creation filled with candy and treasures. I had never seen a piñata before and thought how fun it would be to swing the stick until all sorts of treats and goodies rained down on me. I decided if I could ever have a piñata, I would like it to be in the shape of the princess Cinderella, although then I might not want to break it open because it would be so pretty.

In late adolescence, I began adding layers of papier-mâché to my own life, trying to create something that looked like a treasure-filled princess instead of a welfare girl wearing hand-me-downs.

With six children and a welfare budget, my mom couldn't afford to buy us the brand names that many of my friends wore, so I eagerly accepted them from friends who had outgrown them. Today, when I look at an eighth-grade school photo, I see a smiling girl with long, wavy brown hair. I am wearing my favorite clothes for picture day: a pair of gray corduroy culottes with a matching vest, and a striped cowl-neck sweater.

The culottes came from my friend Holly. She handed them to me, along with other treasured pieces of clothes in a brown paper sack. I was thrilled to get them because Holly also had a tiny frame, and they fit me perfectly. When I received coveted Levi jeans from another friend, Terry, I would have to wear a pair of sweatpants underneath them to make them fit because she had already developed curves. I didn't mind the discomfort if they made me look like my friends.

I had unwittingly started my papier-mâché creation. I looked almost normal. But I knew it was an illusion. *If I was broken open, nothing sweet or valuable would come pouring out because aside from shame and fear, I was empty. A wasteland. Best not let anyone see inside,* I thought.

I pretended in school and with my friends, but at home, I was sullen. I slammed cupboards doors and sent scathing looks towards my mother, her boyfriend, and her other friends who sat around drinking whiskey in the middle of the day.

My journal of poetry from that time reads: *You see my smile and never know it is a tear painted yellow. You hear my laughter and never realize it is a scream skating backwards.*

I hated that everyone knew my mother was unwed and pregnant. But that hate turned into something different the moment my mom returned home from the hospital with my new sister, Jessie.

I instantly fell in love with the tiny newborn.

The whole family was smitten with our beautiful little infant, and my sisters and I fought to take care of her. She was the most precious thing I had ever seen. Choosing outfits for her was more fun than dressing Barbie dolls had been with my friend Becky when I was younger.

I assumed my mom would settle down and go on the wagon, as we called her seasons of sobriety. After all, she had a baby to care for now. I didn't know what was happening in her heart, but as far as my twelve-year-old mind could tell, she didn't change at all.

My mother wasn't just beautiful, she was also witty and kind. She had a generous heart towards people and a gift for hospitality. People were drawn to her.

She was also an alcoholic.

I could always tell when she was first getting lit. Her sparkly, mischievous dark brown eyes would turn glassy, and her words would slide into each other. Her favorite drink was Canadian Club and Pepsi. But sometimes she drank Kahlua and milk, which was much heavier. When she would get full, she often stumbled to the bathroom, stuck her finger down her throat, and forced herself to throw up so she could continue drinking.

I wanted to scream at her, tell her she was worth so much more than the way she was treating herself. I wanted her to know what it was doing to all of us, but the words would get stuck inside of me, as though my vocal cords had frozen.

Our family, like many in the 70s and 80s, simply didn't talk to one another about messy issues. With no place to go, the feelings of anger and shame and bitterness grew inward. So did feelings of impotence.

Mom, with her heart for people, often invited folks she met at bars to our apartment, and they would sit around drinking, smoking cigarettes, and listening to country music albums. I despised their drunken laughter, the blaring country music, and the clouds of smoke from the Winston or Salem or Pall Mall cigarettes that dangled from their mouths.

I hated that, once again, I never knew what I would come home to after school or who I would find at our house in the morning.

Once, a respectable boy from school called and asked to talk to me. I knew what he wanted. He was calling to ask me to go to an upcoming dance with him. My friends and his friends had forewarned me. I told my mom I didn't want to talk to the boy.

"Tell him I'm not home," I told her.

A few moments later she came back to my bedroom. "What's the matter with you? Do you think you are too @#$%&! good to go out with him?" I was shocked by her scornful tone, and I didn't respond. But when she turned around and left, I wanted to shout after her: "No, Mom, I'm not good enough. That's what I think. *I'm not good enough.*"

My communication with my mom remained inward, and I rarely shared what I felt or thought. Instead, I sulked. I slammed more cupboards. I glared. It was ineffective communication because I didn't even know what I was trying to say.

Two of my mother's closest friends were Hazel and Cathy from the apartments upstairs. Hazel had one blue eye and one brown eye, hair on her chin, and a tender heart. When she drank, she became sweet and mushy. She'd hold out her arms, motion for a hug, and then squeeze me against her generous body before I could respond.

Cathy, the other upstairs neighbor, was tall and reed thin. She had two daughters and a volatile relationship with her redheaded, Canadian boyfriend, Reggie. I often babysat for Cathy, staying long hours with her children when she went out. I would fight to stay awake. I read every story in the romance magazines, *True Story* and *True Romance*, that she kept around. My eyes would be dry and achy when, like my mother, she returned in the wee hours of the morning. Like my mom, Cathy received food stamps, and she used them to pay me. It was okay, I thought, because I wasn't worth real money anyways. And I could buy as many Marathon chocolate bars as I wanted.

I liked Cathy and Hazel, but I longed for my mom to have sober friends.

One day, when I was around eleven years old, Mom crossed the border to party with friends other than our upstairs neighbors. I spent the day riding my bike through town, and eventually down the steep hill to the town's playground. I pedaled fast, loving the wind in my face, as I sang the lyrics that I knew to Waylon Jennings' "Good Hearted Woman." I mused over the notion of a woman loving a man so much that she overlooked his "good timing ways" and wondered whether that was a smart thing. Lost in the song's mystery, I hit a rock and found myself sprawled on the dirt road. On the way down, I slammed into the middle frame of my bike, and I could feel wetness in my pants. Wincing, I trudged home, pushing the bike beside me. I threw my bike down in the apartment building's shared front yard and headed to my bedroom for a change of clothes. It felt as though I had peed my pants. I was shocked and scared when I saw blood. I paced around my room for a few minutes, feeling excruciating pain in my lower region. Not knowing what else to do, I walked up the stairs to Hazel's apartment. The door was ajar, and it was obvious that she and her friends had been drinking. Despite the alcohol, she was keen enough to know that something was wrong.

"Whatsa matter?" she crooned. There were several other people in her apartment and shyness seized me. I fidgeted, wishing I had stayed home. "You can tell me, Sweetie. Whatsa matter? Here, come give ole Hazel a hug and tell me what's wrong." Hazel pulled me towards her, squeezing me with arms that jiggled when she moved them. She patted me on the head and turned my face towards hers. "Whatsa matter? C'mon, you can tell me."

I whispered the words. "I'm bleeding."

"You're bleeding? Where?" She pushed me back a bit and looked me over. I glanced around the room then leaned back in.

"In my private area." I could barely look at her, but when I did, her confused face suddenly lit up.

"Oh, honey, you started your period!" She clapped her hands and the other women in the room squealed and began congratulating me as though I had won a prize.

"You're a woman now," the women said as they all hugged me.

I knew they were wrong. I knew the bleeding had to do with the bicycle accident, but Hazel was already asking Cathy for some Stayfree maxi pads for me and giving me instructions for using them, and as usual I couldn't find my words.

I took the pads and threw them away when I got home, shoving them to the bottom of the trash can even though I knew they cost money that shouldn't be wasted and I might need them. Later I lay in bed unable to sleep, in pain from injuries that would appear to heal within the week, only to resurface decades later. That night the bleeding stopped, but resentment at my mother for once again not being there when I needed her continued to fester.

Eventually, we moved out of the apartment on Province Street into a rental house about a ten-minute walk away. The rental was small–with just two bedrooms–but I thought of it as a mansion compared to what we had been living in. It was a *house*. A single-family dwelling. We had a front and backyard that we didn't have to share. We had a garage, which gave us an extra place to hang out since my mom didn't own a car. I liked that I could still walk to school. And I loved our new neighbors. So many amazing changes.

What didn't change, however, was my mom's habit of meeting people at the bars and inviting them back to our house when the bars closed.

And my continued anger about that. Especially after she became friends with an old man named Gary. Stooped and gray haired, Gary had a wrinkled and weathered face that seemed to fit his apelike walk. For a season he was a frequent visitor to our home. I'm sure like many men he was enchanted with my mom, her beauty, and her magnetic personality. But something about him made me afraid to meet his eyes.

Gary always arrived at our house with a brown bag filled with either Canadian Club or Kahlua for my mom and treats for us kids—usually candy bars and potato chips. I hated myself for devouring his pitiful offerings, for eagerly accepting his attempts to befriend us. I wished I had enough control to resist them. I longed to throw the Doritos and Reese's Pieces back at him. Instead, I greedily wolfed them down and wished there was more, a prelude to my own increasingly out-of-control season.

One night, as I was coming out of my upstairs bedroom, Gary was on the stairs heading up to use the bathroom. It seemed strange. Most of the time he used the bathroom downstairs. As he started to pass me, he grabbed my arms and stuck his tongue in my mouth. He pressed his body against mine and shoved his tongue in further. Shocked, I couldn't move at first. Finally, I pushed him off me and ran back to my room. I slammed the door and sat on my bed, shaking. After a while, I heard him stumbling back down the stairs, where my mother was drinking her Kahlua, and Kenny Rogers belted out lies in some stupid love song.

I went into the bathroom and vomited.

Even now, I struggle to understand, to put into words, how this one moment affected me. For decades I told myself I was overreacting. *It wasn't like Gary raped you. Quit your bawling*, I lectured myself. But the truth was that this old man's tongue in my mouth, his breath on my face, his body touching mine without permission, had a deep psychological impact on me. I felt violated, and dirtier than ever.

Rage sprouted from those emotions, particularly rage at my mother. For some reason, I blamed her. It was her fault that this man was in our house; it was her fault for being drunk. I loved my mother fiercely, but there were many times when anger and bitterness braided themselves so tightly in with the love that it became almost impossible to separate them.

The earlier seeds of self- hatred that began when her former boyfriend spoke sexually explicit things to me now grew into a forest of emotions, and I couldn't find my way out of the darkness. Once again, I felt power-less, impotent. Like I had no control over what happened to me. I had nightly dreams where I would find myself half awake and aware of my surroundings but paralyzed and unable to scream for someone to help me. These awake dreams terrified me, and they continued for more than a decade.

I began to search for ways to be in control. I thought I found the answer in a twisted friendship with bulimia nervosa. At first, I didn't know the official name for the dangerous eating and purging pattern, just that it was a way I could maintain a sense of power on the days when I stuffed my emotions beneath layers of junk food. I was hoodwinked.

Instead of gaining control, I was losing it.

PART TWO:

LOSING CONTROL

The Mirror (1983)

I glance at my reflection
But I do not recognize the face.
"Liar!" I scream over and over
But I am only deceiving myself
Mirrors do not lie
I lash out and the mirror shatters
Pieces are everywhere
I drop to my knees
And the glass pierces my skin
I feel nothing
It is the sharpest pain of all

4: Hoodwinked

SITTING ON THE FLOOR IN FRONT OF THE TOILET, I watched the red chunks swirl around the porcelain bowl before disappearing. Eventually, I stood up and rinsed my mouth trying to get rid of the taste of pizza and stomach acid. It lingered in my nose, my mouth, in every part of me. But at least the pizza itself was gone from my body.

I shouldn't have eaten so much after soccer practice, I scolded myself.

At first, I'd been hungry, but then I couldn't seem to stop myself from shoving the stringy, cheesy pizza slices in my mouth even after my stomach felt stretched and full. Like my mother, I had learned to stick my finger down my throat. But not so I could keep drinking. For me it was about gaining control over undisciplined eating. I knew that if I wanted to keep my papier-mâché princess image, I couldn't allow myself to gain weight.

My older sister and brother were both athletic and smart. I still felt clumsy and inept, like I would never measure up to their outgoing personalities. Even back when my fifth-grade teacher, Mr. Lehrbaum, wrote on my report card "Marie's creative writing is outstanding!" my self-limiting beliefs would not let the words sink in. I had already accepted that there was nothing good, nothing of value, inside of me, and by the time I entered high school this false belief had become an anchor to which I was moored.

43

I had once heard a friend of my father say that I was cute. Now, as a teenager, I decided that if I could *appear* cute, if I could continue to make the outside look like a papier mâché princess, then the hollowness of the piñata wouldn't matter so much. I knew I would have to work hard at creating that image and maintaining my weight, and I would have to keep smiling despite the emptiness inside. It would be difficult, but it would be worth it.

I was a freshman in high school when I discovered the false hope of bulimia. At first, I only threw up occasionally. I thought no one would notice. I wasn't as discreet as I thought.

One day my older sister looked at me in my white painter's pants and accused me of being anorexic. In my distorted thinking, I wished she was right. I thought anorexia was so much cooler than bulimia, but I didn't have the self-control to say no to food, couldn't even get an eating disorder right. So rather than starve myself, I threw up what I ate. And I looked thin in my white painter's pants.

Eventually, I was throwing up at least once a day and trying unsuccessfully to avoid food the rest of the time.

One day, during my sophomore year of high school, I arrived home from school and carried my stack of books up to my room. I found a newspaper clipping on my bed. It was about teen girls and eating disorders. I assumed my mother had put it there since nobody else was home. But my mother and I never talked about it, and I continued forcing myself to throw up until I married my husband years later.

During those high school years, I also stepped into the miry clay of alcohol addiction.

I was only in eighth grade when beer and liquor first began to woo me. I easily fell for the false promises that they could make me someone new, someone funny, popular, acceptable. I have only a fuzzy recollection of the events of the night it started, but my friend Anny told me about it the next day.

"Chug, chug, chug!"

I tipped my plastic cup back, ignoring the horribly bitter taste of beer, and then held the cup out for a refill. I reveled in the camaraderie and attention of the popular kids from our high school as they stood around the keg, cheering me on.

I was spending the night at my friend Anny's house. Beautiful and animated, Anny had a figure that caught the boys' attention. She was dating an upperclassman and had invited me to go to a party with her. It was exhilarating. I was noticed, and for once I had no feelings of shame, awkwardness, or defectiveness. I felt free. I felt part of the in-crowd. Even after vomiting half the night while listening to Anny get chewed out by her French-speaking mother for corrupting me, I knew that I was going to party again. Dry heaves, headache, nausea, and a foggy memory seemed a small price to pay for acceptance.

I didn't see that I had stepped into the very lifestyle I hated watching my mother live, the one I had judged her for. I thought I had found an answer for the internal pain and depression, but alcohol preys on broken people. I was only four feet, eleven inches tall and weighed around ninety-five pounds when I began my freshman year. By the time I was a senior in high school, I was drinking most days. It is a miracle that I never suffered alcohol poisoning.

Alcohol was a deceptive friend. It lured me in with whispers of fun and popularity but turned out to be just another controlling back-stabber. Along with inhibitions, it took away memory, good judgment, money, and time. It destroyed my vow to be in control of my life as an adult. Alcohol stood as my taskmaster for years. I hated the things I did during its reign in my life, but I couldn't stop drinking. Under its influence, I lied. I stole. I cheated. And under its influence, I put myself in horrible situations.

One night, I agreed to go to dinner with Michael, my boyfriend at the time. He was a nice enough guy. He was attractive. Intelligent. Held in high esteem by other students at our school. But I was not emotionally healthy enough to date anyone. I wanted out of the relationship. Still, I agree to dinner because he had alcohol.

I was seventeen. I'd barely started my period. Despite my other out-of-control behaviors, I was still a virgin. Though many of my friends had been having sex for years, I had intentionally avoided it. Not out of any kind of desire for moral purity, but because it terrified me.

I knew that when I found the courage, I was going to break up with Michael, so I really didn't want to go to dinner. But I also knew that the date would include alcohol—we almost always drank—and that was a stronger force than wanting to avoid time with him.

That night, alone in his sister's apartment, the two of us sat on the sofa, and he began to kiss me. Things quickly got out of control. Like so many times in the past, my vocal cords wouldn't work. Even inebriated, all the weeping and shouts of no were internal. Afterwards, I blamed myself for this unwanted and unexpected loss of my virginity. I knew I shouldn't have agreed to the date, but I wanted to get drunk. Of course it was my fault, I was the defective one.

That night broke me even more than I already was, and afterwards I didn't care about my reputation. Promiscuity was added to my list of dangerous behaviors. I smiled outwardly but sadness and depression filled the hollow places inside. I was still living the tear-painted-yellow, scream-skating-backwards life I had written about in my poetry journal.

I kept on drinking. And hating myself. And adding layers of papier-mâché to cover the shame. Atop of the layers of pretense, I glued other pieces of self-protection. Self-degradation felt safe. I believed if I put myself down then others couldn't do it.

It seemed safe, seemed like it would protect me and make me more likeable, but this self-belittling just made my friends uncomfortable, as I would learn decades later when I visited my childhood town.

In the late summer of 2021, my husband and I took a trip to Vermont. My mother had passed away in 2012, and I had not returned to my native state since then. But now, despite—or maybe because of—the Covid-19 pandemic, I wanted to see my father before any more time went by.

On a cloudless sunny morning, Scott and I strolled through my small hometown. Ghosts of years past walked behind me, leaning over my shoulder, and whispering remembrances. We crossed an old green bridge, a metal banner welcoming us to Richford, Vermont. I had crossed that bridge over a murky part of the Missisquoi River thousands of times in my youth.

Holding my husband's hand while the humidity caused sweat to trickle down our necks, I realized this was the first time I ever crossed the town bridge feeling like I wanted to throw my arms up and dance, the first time I ever crossed it feeling as light as the still-green maple leaf floating in front of me, the first time feeling completely free from future fears or past regrets.

Like many cities and towns, Richford has run-down areas, and contrasting areas so stunning it makes your heart ache. On the other side of the bridge, we turned a corner and wandered past boarded-up storefronts and graffiti-laden brick walls. Within minutes we reached Province Street. I paused, caught up in nostalgia, remembering the blood stains from George's suicide attempt. Walking down the street to Sonya's house for sleepovers. Exchanging refund bottles for Marathon bars.

The sight of our old apartment building also brought to my mind the best Christmas gift I had ever received—a plastic, yellow record player, and how I escaped life through endlessly playing albums by the Eagles, Air Supply, Abba, and Kenny Rogers. The nostalgia ushered in such an old familiar ache that I squeezed Scott's hand to ground me in the present.

The apartment building still sagged, but now it wore a stained white coat and sighed a forlorn dirge. I had a strange urge to run and pound on doors, to shout, "It's going to be okay! Life will be beautiful, don't give up!" Instead, I kept walking.

We passed the small plot of land on Hillside Terrace where my mom had lived in a run-down mobile home with the man she married after I left home. It was the place where Scott had met my mother, the home where she had nonchalantly handed us porn videos to watch during the first night of our visit.

As Scott and I walked that road more than three decades later, I pieced together memory fragments of small-town life into a bigger picture for him. I spoke about working in the tiny country club at the golf course, and we laughed as I shared a memory of burning eggs for customers one morning while my head throbbed from a hangover. I confessed to him about stealing liquor from the club once when I was partying with friends. "We'd run out of booze and all the stores were closed," I explained. My boss at the country club was the kind man who had rented the little house to my mom during my high school years, and I lugged the guilt of that theft and betrayal around for eons.

I told my husband about weekends spent driving through the town and parking at the old train station, of downing Boones Farm with friends, and adding our intoxicated voices to Bruce Springsteen, John Cougar, Foreigner, REO Speedwagon, or whoever else blared from the speakers.

Scott allowed me to reminisce freely, occasionally interjecting a question, sharing a thought. I told him details about a car accident during my junior year of school. My friend Kadri, her boyfriend, Don, and I had been partying before Kadri got behind the wheel. That was not unusual for young folks in our little town. We cruised the small-town streets with the car windows down and our spirits as carefree and wild as the breeze that whipped our hair about. Carefree and invincible until the moment Kadri lost control of her small Ford. The car flipped several times and when the screams stopped, I found myself against the rear windshield, with blood on my face.

One of the first responders to the scene told us it was miraculous that there were no serious injuries. I came through the experience with nothing more than a few stitches and some soreness. When the tiny threads were snipped and removed, a red squiggly scar remained just beneath my eyebrow. Like my childhood memories, it eventually faded into a barely perceptible line, a mark that could be seen only upon close examination.

But my mother initially saw it as a huge disfigurement—and perhaps an opportunity.

"We should sue Kadri's family," she told me. "You are going to be scarred for life. And they have insurance."

"No, Mom, no!" I pleaded with her. "I'm the one who provided the liquor!"

She didn't pursue the issue, and I was relieved. The humiliation would have been unbearable. And I wondered how she could be so concerned about a tiny scar on my face while being oblivious to the huge scars her lifestyle had inflicted on my heart.

During that same visit back to Vermont in 2021, I reconnected with a high school girlfriend, Rossie Charron. Time had made her even prettier than she was in our teen years and seeing her brought back a flood of remember-whens. I recalled how much I wanted her to be my friend, and even more, how much I had wanted to *be* her. Of course, I'd also wanted to be my boisterous, confident friend Diane. Or Kelly, with the best Gunne Sax dresses and a small family who easily displayed their love and adoration for each other. Or Dee, with her artistic flair and creative personality. Anny with her beautiful face and eye-catching figure.

I guess I wanted to be anybody but me.

Now, decades later, Rossie and I planned a dinner out with some of our other high school friends. Scott and I were some of the last to arrive. We drove right past the old New England house that had been converted to the Phoenix restaurant. When we finally found it, I introduced Scott to my friends and then we slid into a couple of open seats. It was a bitter-sweet time of recounting days past and days present.

During a moment when others were peering over photos of children and grandchildren, Rossie leaned across the table and whispered to me that she had saved some of the notes and letters that I had written to her while we were still in school.

"Oh my gosh! I would love to see them!" I told her.

"I could make copies and send them to you," she offered. "Or if you are back in Richford this week you could pick them up."

After some back-and-forth conversation, we decided that Scott and I would stop by her house before we returned to Colorado, so we could spend some more time catching up and she could give me the written wisps of the girl I once was.

It was late in the afternoon when Scott and I arrived at the Charron's home, and after introducing our husbands—her Reme and my Scott—Rossie led us to her back deck. An array of cheeses, crackers, water, wine, and beer were spread out on a little table, a hospitable offering to a renewed friendship. When Reme drew my normally quiet husband into conversation, Rossie and I slipped away to retrieve the high school ramblings. She handed me a Ziplock bag filled with envelopes bearing my tiny, neat, penmanship.

Fingering the plastic bag, my emotions got caught in a tug of war. Pulling on one side of the rope was eagerness, a desire to be taken back to the days when friends slipped each other handwritten notes rather than sending a quick text. Tugging on the other side of the rope, with an equally strong but slightly painful grip, stood hesitancy, a reticence to look back at the mishmash of emotions, insecurities, and flaws—perceived and otherwise—that might be revealed in my words.

Many of the notes were folded into the shape of an envelope and addressed like they were to be sent through the post office though I remember passing them up and down rows of desks when the teacher's back was turned, and hoping that we wouldn't be caught. A few of the letters did bear an actual postage stamp, from days when Rossie had moved out of state for a brief period, and we stayed in touch through mail.

Both delight and sadness rolled over me as I carefully unfolded and then quickly read through a couple of the letters. I felt a literal jolt from the juxtaposition of a sad, young girl meeting her grown up, joy-filled self. There was laughter in the reminiscing, in remembering the silly nicknames we had for each other: Agatha and Corabelle, Larry and Moe from the Three Stooges.

My friend and I talked and giggled like teenagers about a boy that we had secretly called Space Cadet and pretended we had a crush on. We had teased him but not in a cruel or mean way.

I winced, however, as I recognized in those faded handwritten pages an occasional mean-streak and how my insecurities and self-loathing showed up as jealousy, self-deprecating talk, or criticizing girls whom I envied. There was one girl I mentioned often in my notes to Rossie. Casey was not only a basketball star, she was also smart, her parents doted on her, and her father was a member of the school board. Casey's family was everything my family was not.

I was jealous that Casey and Rossie were good friends, and that they had been friends long before I came along. In those notes I could see that I often put Rossie in an uncomfortable position by venting about Casey to her while also putting myself down. When Casey scored the most points in a basketball game, I would find something about her to criticize. When she returned from a vacation in Florida, thin and brown, I spoke disdainfully of what I considered her boasting nature.

I purposely tried to create division between my friends, and it put Rossie in a hard place. Reading through those old notes, I cringed at words like "*as you know my house isn't like the Bellrose Mansion, but I would love for you to come over to spend the night.*" I believed if I pointed out my deficiencies before someone else could do so, it would be a protective buffer. But it never helped me feel any better.

If I could, I would go back and tell the adolescent and teenage Marie not to worry so much. I would tell her that the value of a person has nothing to do with a house or a brand of clothing. That even when friends couldn't spend the night because they knew about her mother's drinking, it didn't mean she was defective or that she should feel shame for her existence. I would tell her to stop believing lies and live out the truth of who she was, of who she is.

But I didn't know those things back then, and instead of nurturing a close friendship with Casey, and all the beauty that would have come with that, I compared and found myself lacking. So I looked for ways to manipulate and choreograph situations. Envy pulled the strings.

The summer between my junior and senior year of high school, I worked in the administration office at our high school. One of my tasks was to look at students' list of desired courses and create schedules. Whenever possible, I put Casey and I in different classes and tried to put my favorite friends in classes with me. It was another fruitless attempt to control relationships, and it didn't change anything.

The 2021 visit with Rossie was bittersweet. The difference between my life when I lived in that little New England town and now was stunning, and I felt gratitude for where God had brought me.

For weeks after the Vermont visit, I found myself continuing to reflect on my journey.

5: Running Away from Me

BACK IN MY TEEN YEARS WHILE ATTENDING OUR SMALL-TOWN HIGH SCHOOL, one person who noticed something amiss was my French teacher, Ms. Gaudreau. A thin, blond-haired woman with a tiny, pixie nose, Ms. Gaudreau taught Parisian French. I took her class for a few years, but when the partying became more of a priority, and the depression gained a tighter grip, I quit.

One day Ms. Gaudreau stopped me in the hall. "How are you doing?" she asked.

"Fine." I started to move past her, but her words stopped me.

"You used to dress so nice." Her words were a statement, but I could hear the questions standing behind them.

"I'm late for Latin," I said, pressing past her. Instead of Latin class, I went into the girls' bathroom and stared at myself in the mirror. Despite the bulimia, I was beginning to gain weight, and I covered the pudginess with looser clothing. I looked tired. I splashed water on my face and turned away from my reflection.

An almost identical conversation happened with Ms. Gaudreau a few months later, but the second time I responded in anger. "I'm fine," I snapped, and she looked taken aback. At lunch I complained to my friends. "She's such a stuck up, nosey %@$&*" I told them. Underneath my bravado was a choking fear that my carefully hidden inner mess was leaking out.

Another time, Mr. Labier, a popular teacher who was chaperoning one of our school dances, sent me home from the dance. I was so drunk I could barely stand, and I was sobbing over some things my mom—who was having a party with her friends—had said to me before I left. He could have reported me, and I could have been suspended. Instead, he made sure I had a ride home and forced me to look him in the eye. "Look, I know something is going on. Go home, sober up, and talk to someone."

I sobered up, but not for long. And I didn't talk to anyone. The closest I came was sharing some of my dark poetry with Mr. LaClair, my creative writing teacher. His genuine love of students was evident in the way he related to us, the way he saw our potential. Sometimes he came to class with his guitar slung over his shoulder and played folk or bluegrass songs, reminding us that lyrics were a powerful form of creative expression. I remember the earnest way he shoved his wire spectacles on his nose and bounced a bit on his feet while talking passionately about Joni Mitchell, Bob Dylan, and poetry; the way he created a sense of safety for young people to express themselves.

I shared my own poetry with him, and I'll never forget his encouragement, his ardent response. "You're good." He told me. "I mean, really good, Marie. I don't often see this caliber in young people." He continued, "You need to do something with this gift. The emotion is gripping."

His last statement had a quizzical tone, an invitation to share more. But I didn't know how to do that. I didn't know what to say. For a while I held onto his words. It was the first time I'd been told I had a *gift*, but the other words I heard in my head, the ones that said I would never measure up, drowned them out, melted them into a puddle that couldn't be solidified again. I didn't know how to find my voice, but what I did know was that I was sinking fast and if something didn't change, I would drown beneath the quicksand of myself.

The summer between my junior and senior year of high school, I met with an Air Force recruiter, and in October of 1984, after I graduated, I headed to Lackland Air Force Base in Texas. I learned from the recruiter that there would be no alcohol during basic training, and I thought that would be my salvation.

But changing my environment without inward healing was simply a new setting for my old patterns. I should have felt brave. I should have felt proud of myself for stepping out into the unknown. I should have felt excited about starting anew. Instead, I shoved all the self-loathing and shame right into my duffle bag and carried it onto every bus and every airplane that took me further away from Vermont. First I went to basic training in Texas, then Tech School in Colorado, and my first PCS (permanent change of station) at Sembach Air Base in Germany.

The time passed in a kaleidoscopic, drunken blur.

The memories of my PCS in Germany are fuzzy, but I know that I went through men faster than a creemee melts on a ninety-degree day. I drank nearly every night, despite waking up each morning sweating from a blanket of shame and regret, and vowing, "I'm not going to drink today."

Once, I called my boss and told him I couldn't find my security badge to get on the flightline for work. I hadn't sobered up from the night before, and sensing more than a lost badge, Ssgt. Appletree came to my dormitory room to check on me. He saw the beer bottles and trash everywhere and noted my obvious hangover. He had no choice but to write a disciplinary report on me. I received an official Air Force Letter of Reprimand.

In the past, I had been tidy and wanted everything in its place, but I was spiraling, losing control of even the little things I did to give myself an illusion of being in charge. I cleaned my dorm room after Ssgt. Appletree left that day, but I remained a mess. The bulimia continued. The drinking continued. The self-loathing continued.

During my first October in Germany, my father decided to come visit me so he could experience a real Oktoberfest.

At that time, I had conflicting emotions about my father. I didn't know his own history. I didn't know about his abusive father who beat his mother and abandoned his family when my father was just nine years old. I didn't know about his own experiences with poverty and being on state aid. I didn't know about all the jobs he had before and after school to help with family finances. I didn't know about the motorcycle accident that had left him hospitalized for months, or that when he was in the military, he had sent most of his monthly pay checks home to support his single mother. I didn't know about the first wife who had cheated on him.

He didn't communicate any of this to me until I was thirty-eight years old. The heartfelt note he wrote to me and my siblings in 2004 shared bits and pieces of his life and ended with "It's been hard for me to show love, but it has always been there."

By then I had been married for seventeen years. I had six children. By then—even before my father shared the painful details of his past—I had discovered that he had many admirable qualities and I knew that he would be there for me no matter what.

But back in my early military days, in October of 1985, I knew very little about the man I called Dad. Instead of talking to him—which terrified me—I shoved my emotions and thoughts and questions deep down inside.

The fact that he was coming to visit me and there wouldn't be any other family around to make conversation or carry the bulk of the visit was overwhelming. I didn't allow myself to think about it. I pretended it wasn't really going to happen, so when my father arrived, I had not even made reservations for him in Billeting, the base military lodging.

The first night of his arrival, we slept in the lobby.

During that time in my life, I suffered frequent blackouts, but I know we made it to Oktoberfest and drank until I could barely stand. We traveled to Paris and experienced the Moulin Rouge, had caricatures done as we wandered the Champs-Elysée, took photos in front of the Eiffel Tower, and viewed the Mona Lisa. We explored the Bavarian Forest and toured Neuschwanstein castle. which is rumored to be the inspiration for Walt Disney's castle.

It should have been a great father-daughter bonding time., but I don't think either one of us was capable of bonding.

On the last night of my dad's visit, we were out partying with some of my friends who were stationed at a different base. My girlfriends loved my father. He bought them drinks, danced with them, and flirted like he was a twenty-year-old. I watched one of my girlfriends sit on my father's lap and throw her head back in laughter at something he said.

I didn't get it. I didn't even know how to talk to him. I kept chugging glass after glass of vodka and orange juice as though I would find some revelation at the bottom of a drink. The next thing I remember, I was waking up in a friend's dorm room where I had passed out. Other bodies were sprawled around on the floor and chairs and a sofa. As I tried to stop the room from spinning, I realized what had awakened me. A strange guy was trying to take my pants off. I kicked at him and tried to cry out, hoping my father would wake up and help me, but I didn't even know which lump in the room, if any, was him.

I pulled myself off the couch and stumbled around the bodies until I found the door. I managed to make it to the room of one of my few non-drinking friends and pounded on her door. "I'm coming, I'm coming already." I heard the annoyance in her sleepy voice before her door opened a crack. My friend took one look at me and threw open her door to let me in.

Later that day, without even saying goodbye to my father before he flew back to the states, I took a bus back to the base, vowing to myself that I would quit drinking and get control of my life.

But that time with my father sparked some deep depression, and instead of drinking less, I began drinking more.

A few weeks later, after an out-of-control night at the NCO Club, I sat, alone, on the bed in my dormitory room, still hating my life and myself. I thought I had left that back in Vermont, but now I knew it was inside of me. I glared across the room where a crystal wine decanter, matching shot glasses, long stemmed champagne glasses, and shorter, fatter wine glasses sat on a dresser. I had been collecting the crystal pieces for months. But now, in my drunken stupor, they taunted me.

Who do you think you are? they seemed to mock. *You'll never be a crystal wine decanter kind of person. You are nothing.*

I crossed the room, picked up each piece of crystal and threw it against the wall, watching as one by one the beautiful vessels shattered into sparkling fragments on my carpet. Rage welled up in me, but I didn't know what I was raging against. Emotionally spent, I passed out on the floor.

The next morning, I stared at the shattered glass. My stomach reeled, my eyes were puffy and red, and I knew I could not possibly make it into work on time. I dressed in my wrinkled fatigues and stumbled to sick call, certain that I would be excused from the day's duties. I couldn't wait to crawl back into bed, pull the covers over my head, and disappear. I'd been down the sick-call road before. But this time was different. The doctor didn't rush me through my appointment. Her no-nonsense demeanor would not accept my get-out-of-jail free card. She said she could tell I was still drunk. She began to ask probing questions. Personal questions that crashed through my walls of silence. I broke down, in my not-yet-sober state, and puked out the words of anger and confusion and self-loathing that I had shoved down for decades. Instead of sending me back to my dorm room to sleep it off, I heard the doctor talking to someone on the phone.

The next thing I knew, I was checking into the psychiatric ward of Landstuhl Medical Hospital. I sobered up fast. I found myself in a hospital gown, in a room with several people who clearly had mental health issues. One woman with frizzy blond hair wandered the room, touching walls, and mumbling to herself. Another sat in a corner rocking back and forth and occasionally spewing out vulgar profanity.

The possibility that I could be staying in this place for days or weeks terrified me. I don't remember sleeping. What I do remember is paperwork: questions, evaluations, and more questions. An entire day of meeting with doctors and clinicians. Interviews and talks and filling in bubbles on page after page.

The following afternoon, the powers that be told me I could go home. In their blind wisdom, they decided that I didn't have a mental health issue. I was merely a drunk. The military required me to attend a year of weekly meetings as part of a substance abuse program, but other than that, I was considered fit as could be and released.

I called Master Sergeant Butler, my boss from the jet engine shop where I worked in a supply administrative position. Embarrassed and ashamed, but trusting his kind nature, I asked if he could come pick me up. I thought of him as weird but gentle giant, a man of great physical stature who seemed to defy physics whenever he unfolded himself from the Mini Cooper he drove. Little did I know that he was a man of faith, and of prayer.

At that moment a real battle for my soul began.

Instead of taking me directly to my dorm, Master Sergeant Butler invited me to his home to meet his wife and two daughters. His three "girls" as he called them, had the most amazing blue eyes. Even more amazing was the way they embraced and accepted me. They built and devoured hot fudge sundaes, laughed, and didn't treat me as someone who had just spent the night in a psych ward. Being in the midst of a loving family, watching the banter and teasing, and witnessing a natural camaraderie that didn't require alcohol to exist was such a foreign experience.

Looking back, it is easy to see that they spent regular time in God's presence and naturally reflected His beauty. The Butlers invited me to go to church with them that weekend. "Sure, I'd like that," I responded, knowing the words, like my life, were an empty lie. By Sunday, I would most likely be in a bar in Kaiserslautern or back at the NCO Club on base. I had no intention of joining them for a religious service.

For the next couple of months, I attended a mandatory substance abuse program midweek and continued drinking on the weekends. I struggled to find worth through physical relationships with men as drunk and lost as me. Meanwhile, at least once a day I waited until the dorm bathroom was empty, locked myself in a stall, and purged myself of unwanted junk food, wishing I could purge all the ugliness of my soul with it.

Behind the scenes, the Butlers and members of their church were praying for me to find love and freedom in Jesus.

One morning not too long after my stay in the Landstuhl hospital, I rushed to the bathroom and didn't need to shove my finger down my throat; I lost my breakfast without even trying.

It happened again, a few days later.

And again.

I had never had regular menstrual cycles. I hadn't started my period until I was almost seventeen, and my mother had immediately put me on birth control. "Just in case," she said. The daily birth control pill had never regulated my cycle like the doctor had said it would, so I had no clue if I was late or not.

I walked over to the base exchange and bought an e.p.t. (early pregnancy test). Unlike today's simple tests with immediate results, this one felt like a chemistry experiment. During the two-hour wait, my emotions flip-flopped more than my stomach had been doing.

What if? What if? What if?

The test was positive.

6: Pregnant

THE RELATIONSHIP I WAS CURRENTLY IN WAS IFFY AT BEST. I told the guy I was pregnant and was shocked by his response. He said he was not ready to be a father and gave me an ultimatum: have an abortion and continue our relationship or choose the baby and be alone. He was clear that it couldn't be both him and the baby.

Surely in response to the prayers of Msgt. Butler and his family, I chose my baby over that relationship. During that season in my life, Msgt. Butler and his family continued to pray. They invited me to church, and at first I made excuses as to why I couldn't join them. They had an answer for every excuse. No car? They would pick me up. No dressy clothes? None needed. Finally, because I still didn't know how to simply say no to anything, I relented.

It wasn't long before I attended a ladies' group at their church for the same reason, not because I was motivated to change my life, but because I couldn't say, "No thanks." In the weekly meetings, some older women taught me to knit. But these ladies, with their clicking needles and gentle, religious dispositions, unnerved me, and I soon stopped going. Before I did, however, Msgt. Butler and his wife gave me a leather Bible with a loving inscription from the two of them. I set it aside, not really knowing what to do with it.

My former boss will never know on this side of eternity how fully his prayers were answered, or what the gift of that Bible came to mean to me. Eventually, that Bible fell apart from use. But not then. It would still be several years before I would surrender my heart to Jesus.

Meanwhile, I was single and pregnant and in a substance abuse program. I still wore a heavy cloak of fear and shame, but as my due date drew closer, a new emotion was beginning to take root: Excitement. I remembered how much I had loved Jessie when she was a newborn, and how I used to pretend she was all mine. Now I wouldn't have to pretend, I would have my own baby to love and care for.

A few months later, I received orders to return to the United States. When I reported to my new base, Hurlburt Field AFB in Florida, I was twenty years old, six months pregnant, exhausted, and scared. I had no idea what the future held. I didn't even have a driver's license. My mom didn't have a car when I was in high school, and I had joined the military without ever getting a license.

Soon I connected with a couple of friends who had left Sembach before I did and were now stationed at the same base in Florida. One of them, Tony, an Italian with a big heart, helped me obtain my license and buy my first car—a used Chevette—just a couple of months before I was due to give birth. I rented a tiny house near the base and settled in.

I hadn't really been in communication with my father since his visit for Oktoberfest, but my mom told me that he planned to come to Florida and see me. "Well, your father says he is going to see you and the baby no matter what," she said after I shared during a phone conversation that I might be driving myself to and from the hospital when I gave birth. That commitment from my father led me to pick up the phone and call him. We made plans for him to arrive a couple of weeks after my due date, so that I would have time to get used to being a mom.

Two weeks after my due date passed, my father and stepmother, Phyllis, arrived at the Pensacola International Airport as planned. I still hadn't given birth and I wondered aloud if I ever would. But just hours after my parents set their suitcases in the spare bedroom of my tiny home, I went into labor. My son's birth was quick and as easy as a delivery can be, and I was able to hold my him right away.

Looking down at the ruddy face staring up at me, I felt my heart double in size. I held his warm little fingers and vowed to be the best mother I possibly could. My newborn, Kyle, became my number-one priority. It crushed me when my six weeks maternity leave came to an end, and I had to return to work.

I still drank, but not the excessive amounts I had consumed in the past. I spent my days in an aircraft supply office located inside a large helicopter hanger. My evenings and nights were consumed with caring for my newborn. The higher-ups in my military squadron decided that the stress of being a single new mom might be too much for me to handle and required me to complete another six months in the substance abuse program.

Stress comes in many outfits. I had worn fear, skittishness, and anxiety since childhood, and as my commanders predicted, this season added another garment of stress. But it wasn't my new baby that brought it about. It was palmetto bugs.

One Saturday evening, after a lengthy chat with my sister, I hung up the phone and turned towards the TV. And I shrieked. A bloodcurdling shriek. Two huge, black insects scuttled up my living room wall from behind the television, their legs making little clicking sounds like knitting needles in the hands of little old ladies.

They were Palmetto bugs I would later learn. Palmetto bugs are hideous insects that look like giant cockroaches on steroids. And they can fly. These ghastly things had taken up residence in my little house. I freaked out. When I turned out the lights, they scurried across the kitchen floor or up the walls. The sound of them scurrying caused my skin to crawl. Because of their speed and the way they seemed to come out of nowhere, I jumped at the slightest movement.

I had lived with fear for decades, and now a new irrational fear grew out of control. Like stress, my fears had many looks. Sometimes it was aggressive and venomous, like a slithering snake injecting its poison and temporarily paralyzing my vocal cords. Other times it was much more subtle, hidden away like a prison bracelet around my ankle, allowing me to wander only so far before sounding an alarm notifying me I needed to return to safety, even if that safety was a mirage.

Most of the time fear was a nameless, shapeless figure loitering in the shadows, just beyond my periphery of understanding, unseen yet totally controlling my life.

So many kinds of fears. The fear of being invisible and the fear of being seen. The fear of the known and the fear of the unknown. The fear of the dark and the fear of venturing out into the light. The fear of change and the fear of things staying the same. Fear of little things like mice in the walls, and bigger things like strangers and single parenting and getting lost while driving. Fear of the tangible and fear of the intangible.

With the Palmetto bugs in Florida, all that fear and anxiety morphed into a *phobia* that would become debilitating over the next few years. The Palmetto bugs upset me so much that I asked my friend Tony to move into the spare bedroom in my little storm cottage. He agreed, probably thinking it would be a whole lot easier than responding every time I called him to come over and deal with bugs. Tony eased some of the single parenting stress by sharing the rent and other household expenses. More important, he became a good friend—and he took care of the palmetto bugs. This helped, but sudden movements still made me skittish. I remained constantly jumpy.

If I could go back and pen my own life story from scratch, I would write myself as an entirely different protagonist than the one I was. I would create a braver version of me, one who needed no rescuing. But the truth was that my life often felt out of control, and I was afraid of so many things. I longed for something or someone to make me different.

When Kyle was three months old, Tony and my childcare provider persuaded me that it wasn't healthy for me to stay home all the time.

"You'll be a better mother if you take some time for yourself. You know, get out and have fun with other adults," Tony encouraged.

Despite misgivings, I dropped Kyle off at his babysitter's house and headed out with Tony to a bar in Fort Walton Beach.

That night changed the course of my life.

PART THREE:
ILLUSION OF CONTROL

Papier Mâché Princess (1996)

A familiar face smiles each Sunday
From her second-row pew
A thrift store soul hides
beneath Calvin Klein and Saks Fifth Avenue
She dangles precariously
knowing with the slightest whisper of the wind
The facade will shatter
Revealing the irony
There are no prizes within
She is just a papier mâché princess
Filled with carefully wrapped pieces of despair
And so she remains
Safely
Suspended
Just
Beyond
Reach.

7: Knight in a Turquoise Shirt

IT HAD BEEN MONTHS SINCE I HAD BEEN IN A BAR, but I quickly put away a couple of Killian Reds. The beers emboldened my timid nature. As I stood talking with Tony and a couple of CH-53 helicopter mechanics from the base, I noticed a quiet, scruffy-bearded man in a turquoise shirt and white pants. I didn't know why he was with the military guys. He was eating Jiffy Pop popcorn, and I suddenly felt ravenous. When he held out the pan, I couldn't resist, and I shoved a handful in my mouth. And then another one. When I finished, I licked the butter and salt off my fingers and looked up into the bluest eyes I had ever seen.

My heart somersaulted. I fell head-over-heels in lust.

Two weeks later, I moved in with Scott, the man in the turquoise shirt.

Turned out he worked in the same hangar that I did and was a well-respected, loved-by-everyone helicopter mechanic who had been on leave for a couple of weeks, which explained the beard and longer hair.

A mere three and a half months after that, we stood in front of a justice of the peace who had remnants of powdered doughnut on her face, and we recited a quick promise to love, honor, and cherish each other no matter what.

We were clueless, just a couple of hung-over, messed-up young people who carried enough junk into the sum of us that we should have imploded, should have been crushed into fragments from the weight of it all.

And we would have, if we had not leaned into the grace of God.

God can take those things that in and of themselves could destroy us and use them for our good. He can do this even before we recognize His hand. He is at work long before we hear of Romans 8:28, which promises that "in all things God works for the good of those who love Him, who have been called according to His purpose." Not that all things *are* good, but God can work good out of all things, including my phobia of palmetto bugs and cockroaches.

Just months after Scott and I recited our wedding vows, we decided Kyle needed a sibling, and in a blink, I held an e.p.t. test confirming what I already knew. I was pregnant again. Although I had recently been awarded the prestigious John Levitow Award at the end of NCO school—which was an indicator that I would likely fast track through the ranks—I finished my current Air Force contract and didn't reenlist. Our second son, Josh, was born four days before Scott and I celebrated our first wedding anniversary.

As the months passed, we felt the crunch of a family of four living off one military income. We applied for base housing—free housing for military personnel—and put Scott's house on the market. We got an offer on his house immediately and moved into a tiny, prefabricated rental just down the road while we crossed our fingers and waited for the military housing office to let us know that a place was available.

The modular home was poorly built. Gaps around windows and doors provided an open invitation for Palmetto bugs, crickets, and other pests. The washer and dryer were in a dark shed off the back of the house. I always stuck my hand inside the door, turned on the light, and then rushed back into the house for a bit before carrying out a basket of laundry. I wanted to give the nocturnal bugs a chance to go into hiding, so I could pretend they weren't there.

I wasn't fooling myself though. I remained as jittery as a caffeine junkie during those days, never knowing when something would go scooting out in front of me. I screamed if a piece of lint brushed against my bare skin. I couldn't wait for the day we could get out of there. But months went by, and the base housing office never contacted us. Our time in the little prefabricated box stretched on for months.

Finally, when Scott was out of town on a temporary duty assignment (TDY), I called military housing. "I'm wondering what is going on. You told us we would have a house long before now, but we haven't had a single call yet." I watched the boys splash in a little plastic pool in the dirt and weed patch that masqueraded as our front yard while I waited for an answer.

"We called SSgt. Isom's work number and left a message, but we never heard back," the office receptionist explained.

"He has been TDY!" I said. My exasperation slipped out before I could stop it. "Why didn't you call our home number?"

"Well, we have an apartment unit available on Struthers Road." The person on the phone side-stepped my question.

"We'll take it," I replied. Struthers Road was known for being in one of the worst housing complexes, but I didn't want to risk waiting for months again.

Meanwhile, back in the foothills of Golden, Colorado, my father-in-law and stepmother-in-law were praying for us. They were praying for us to get into a house on base, yes, but mostly for us to know freedom in Christ. I suspect those prayers led to the phone call we received at the end of that week.

"Hello, is Sgt. Isom there? This is Sgt. Preston from the housing office on Eglin Air Force Base."

I handed the phone to Scott, who had returned from his TDY the day prior, and I chewed on the corner of my finger while he talked. *Please,*

please, please don't let them say that we have to wait longer for a house, I pleaded silently.

"Uh, huh," Scott said. "Okay. Yep. Cool. Thanks."

I couldn't tell much about the conversation from Scott's impassive voice. I pounced on him as soon as he placed the receiver back on its wall-mounted base and started to untangle the cord.

"What did they say? We don't have to wait longer, do we?"

"No," he grinned. "You aren't going to believe this, but they aren't putting us in the house on Struthers. Instead, they're offering us a house that used to be an officer's home. It is a single house with a big yard and community park in the back!"

I squealed. It felt like a miracle. *Why had Housing changed their mind?* I wondered. *Why were they offering us such a jewel of a home?*

Little did we know that God was at work answering prayers we didn't know were being lifted on our behalf.

I couldn't wait to move! I hoped that the new house on Eglin AF Base would finally put an end to my palmetto bug phobia. On a walk-through before our move, I was thrilled to see that the military structure was well built, open, and spacious. Best of all, the washer and dryer were in a large closet off the kitchen. No more venturing out into a dark shed where creepy-crawlies lurked.

I could barely contain my excitement when our moving day arrived. By afternoon, we had all our belongings unloaded from the truck and stacked in our new living room. "Thanks so much!" I waved good-bye to the last of our friends who had helped us put the beds and other furniture together.

"See ya guys soon," Scott added. "We'll plan a party once we are fully unpacked." We tossed empty beer bottles and pizza boxes on top of the already overflowing trash can and plopped ourselves on the couch.

"I love this place already," I smiled at Scott. "The park in the back is going to be great for the boys. But right now, I'm ready for bed."

Kyle and Josh were already asleep, worn out from the excitement and chaos of the weekend move and exploring their new surroundings. After a few minutes Scott and I mustered enough energy to lift ourselves from the couch and headed to the master bedroom, first taking a quick peek at our slumbering boys. We brushed our teeth, undressed, and crawled between the sheets. I sighed and spooned myself into my husband as he switched off the light. I soon reached the beautiful space between wakefulness and sleep, when drowsiness has such a tranquilizing effect that worries, fears and to-do lists simply melt away. It was a short-lived tranquility.

Within moments of turning out the light, I heard it. The distinct and undeniable clicking of roach legs scurrying up the wall. I screamed and Scott fumbled for the light. Sure enough, two of the disgusting black bugs could be seen against the white bedroom wall. Scott managed to kill one, but the other escaped. I kept the light on the rest of the night. I barely slept, envisioning one of the nasty insects crawling on me. Lack of sleep would become a way of life over the next year or two.

The next day, we bought roach bait traps and roach spray. It was the start of what would prove to be a major battle to rid our home of the bugs. No matter how hard we tried, no matter how clean we were, we couldn't conquer them. We hired professional exterminators on a regular basis. We didn't leave so much as a wet spoon in the sink at night. I mopped and swept and disinfected daily. Still they invaded.

The exterminators told us we were dealing with palmetto bugs rather than cockroaches and assured us they didn't take up residence in a home. They lied. The palmetto bugs had staked a claim on our house and refused to give it up. Their presence took a toll on me physically. The lack of sleep and constant jumpiness left me exhausted, which only exacerbated the phobia because I was never at the top of my game cognitively.

After a couple of months, I told Scott I needed to get away. I bought one-way tickets to Vermont for the boys and me, not sure that I ever wanted to return to Florida and its disgusting insects.

While in Vermont, I started seeing a counselor who specialized in phobias. She began desensitization therapy, but I didn't stay in the Green Mountain State long enough to make progress. After a few weeks, I was homesick, not for Florida, and certainly not for the infested house, but for my husband.

Scott made the trek up the East Coast in our little Ford Escort to bring the boys and me back home. During our absence, he had removed kitchen cabinets and sprayed pesticide behind them. Military base exterminators sprayed outside the house and scheduled a fumigation "bombing" to be done after Scott headed north. My sweet husband had even asked a friend to come in and sweep up all the dead bugs before our return, so I wouldn't have to see them.

We arrived home earlier than expected. Exhausted from the long drive with two active toddlers, I couldn't wait to get some sleep. But when I lugged the boys' suitcase through the front door, I immediately spotted upside down palmetto bugs everywhere, some with their legs still twitching. Even worse, some had refused to give up the fight and crawled towards us like snails. Scott dropped the suitcases his was carrying and ran for a broom, I took the boys next door to our neighbors' house and waited for Scott's all clear before returning.

They say phobias are irrational, and I suppose they do appear that way. My fear of the palmetto bugs didn't seem to make sense. Once I posed with a boa constrictor wrapped around my neck while my squeamish friends captured the moment with photos. Yet the comparatively tiny palmetto bugs left me incapacitated. Why would I be so fearful of one but not the other? It seemed irrational.

But when I examined it a little closer, I realized it had to do with control, or the sense of control. With the huge, fat snake, I felt like I was in control. I knew what the situation was and chose to say, "bring it on!"

The palmetto bugs, however, came out of nowhere, much like old Gary in the upstairs hallway back in my teenage years. They made constant and swift appearances that I could not predict, so I was always on guard.

While we adjusted to living in that dream-house-turned-nightmare on Eglin AFB, we got to know our neighbors. One couple, Jeff and Felicia, lived right next door to us. I often ran into Felicia, a pretty blonde with a southern drawl, when I took the boys to the community park. Felicia had two girls the same ages as Kyle and Josh, and some days she accepted my invite to bring her daughters over for lunch. After I washed the colorful Tupperware lunch plates and put them away, Felica and I talked and played Yahtzee while the kids painted, played with Hot Wheels, or stacked blocks.

There was something different about Felicia, but I couldn't figure out what it was. One afternoon I put on some albums, playing music by Styx, Abba, and Crosby, Stills, and Nash. She knew all the words and sang along. "I used to listen to these bands a lot," she said, rolling the dice and penciling in a full house.

"Who's your favorite now?" I asked.

She thought for a moment, then said, "Actually, my favorite bands now are worship bands. Since I gave my life to Christ, worship music just feeds my soul."

In the past, religious people had made me feel uncomfortable. I mocked people who evangelized. One time when Scott and I and a group of friends had staggered out of a bar, a stranger waved a Bible and shouted that we were sinners on our way to hell. We all laughed at him and cheered.

Felicia wasn't like that stranger, accosting us outside of the bar. She never said anything judgmental even though she knew Scott and I spent our weekends partying. But sometimes Scriptures glided out of her mouth as easily and gracefully as an Olympic figure skater. She and her husband, Jeff, often invited us for dinner or barbequed with us at our house. They also regularly invited us to attend church with them on Sunday mornings. We said yes when they invited us, but because we usually ended up drinking on Saturday nights, we never managed to get up in time. We really didn't want to go. Besides, I didn't own a dress, which I assumed to be normal church attire. I felt guilty telling them yes when I knew we likely wouldn't go.

Scott and I continued to battle the roach problem and my phobia, and I wondered if prayer, and a relationship with God, and the spiritual beliefs my new friend had been introducing me to would help me. I was miserable and desperate. She, on the other hand, radiated peace and joy. So I borrowed a cute polka-dot dress with a white lace collar from another neighbor and I convinced Scott we could wake up in time on Sunday morning.

I had no idea what to expect from her church. My parents had been Catholic before they were excommunicated from the church for divorcing, and in Catholic tradition, a priest baptized me as an infant. I had attended catechism classes, made my first confirmation, and sporadically went to Mass.

I wasn't a churchgoer, but even through my drunkest seasons, I believed there was a god and would try to mumble the words to the Our Father, Hail Mary, and Glory Be prayers before passing out. I believed in a god, but I never believed He cared about me or my life. I thought He was "out there somewhere" and if my good works outweighed my bad ones, then I would make it to heaven. I knew I needed to do a lot of good to cancel out all the awful things I had done in the prior years.

Actually, I was afraid to go to church—afraid to face God.

That first Sunday morning at the little church in Niceville, Florida, turned my perspective of God upside-down. I left the service hungry to learn more.

My father-in-law and stepmother-in-law had sent Bibles to Scott and me the year before. I finally began reading mine. We still didn't become churchgoers right away; we continued drinking on Saturday nights and sleeping in on Sundays. But more and more I would find myself knocking on Felicia's door.

"What does the Bible say about drinking? What does the Bible say about parenting? Can God help me with my phobia? Why don't you listen to rock music anymore?" Felicia took in all my random and constant questions with patience, endless cups of freshly percolated coffee, a sense of humor, and a heart full of hospitality.

It turns out that the palmetto-bug-infested house on Eglin AFB was an answer to Scott's parents' prayers because through my struggle with phobia, I developed a deep longing to know this Jesus that my next-door neighbor credited with giving her joy, laughter, passion, and peace.

Soon Felicia and Jeff introduced Scott and me to other young military and civilian families from their church. Like Msgt. Butler's family these people radiated in a way that only those who spend time in God's presence do. These people weren't weirdos like I had always thought religious people were. They weren't boring or "holy rollers." They weren't lacking anything.

Soon, I surrendered my heart and soul to Jesus. Life completely changed.

Sparkling bits of Christ-joy began to fall in and around me. It felt like an explosion of color and light and warmth, like stepping out into a sunny day after decades spent living in a dark basement. I enjoyed game nights with new friends who didn't need alcohol to bring out the deep belly laughter or heart-to-heart conversations. New music filled a hunger I didn't know I had. Teachings from the Word changed my heart and gave me hope. I awoke with joy rather than a hangover. Whatever I gave to God, He refined, restored, and healed.

It was a miraculous season, and I began to believe that nothing ugly would mar my life again. When I put my trust in God, I believed that if

I just did all the right things, I would be protected from hurts and harm. That doing *a* and *b* would and should be followed by *c*. I felt like life was a formula I could conquer.

Yet devastation still reaches God's people. We live in a fallen world, one in which even an innocent night out at a movie theater can end in a horrific massacre. Eventually my illusion would be shattered.

It would be a long journey before I would give God every bit of me—past, present, and future; body, soul, and spirit; hopes, dreams, and passions. It would be a while before I would come to the realization that there are no formulas. Before I would realize that my belief that I could control or manipulate or shape anything—my health, my marriage, my children, my children's health, circumstances—was simply a mirage.

I couldn't control any of it.

Eventually, in realizing these things and coming to a place of letting go of the fight for control, I would be empowered. Eventually, in clinging to Christ and free-falling into grace, I would experience abundance and liberation like I never could have dreamed.

But first would come the shatterings.

8: Shattered Faith

I LOVED MY NEW LIFE. I LOVED BEING A MOTHER TO TWO TODDLER BOYS. I still got butterflies when I looked at my husband. I was surrounded by sunshine and friendships and fellowship. For the first time in my life, I was experiencing personal and spiritual growth in leaps and bounds.

But I hated the palmetto bugs with a passion. So Scott put in for a change of orders and requested an assignment to another base. Because of his career field as a CH-53 helicopter mechanic, and the fact that he was part of a Special Operations Unit, there were not many locations open for transfers. We prayed and waited.

Months later, when Scott came home with official Air Force orders to a military base in England for June of 1991, my squeals of joy brought the boys running, and we shared the news with them. The kids were unimpressed. They nodded indifferently, then headed back to their room for more pressing matters like Hot Wheels and plastic cowboys.

I, on the other hand, couldn't stop grinning and spent the next weeks in a happy-dance mode, even when I started dry heaving in the mornings. I told myself it was from the excitement and anticipation. I ignored the nauseousness. Until I couldn't ignore it.

Just prior to leaving the U.S., I reluctantly bought a pregnancy test and for a third time in my life confirmed what my mornings had been

79

telling me. Our family of four would soon become a family of five. The intensity of the morning sickness for this pregnancy caught me off guard, and I spent most of my time before we left lying around. Whenever I stood up, it felt like I had been riding a fast-spinning merry-go-round after a night of drinking.

This relentless morning sickness made the move to a new country challenging. I couldn't even keep liquids down, and the day we arrived in the UK I was hospitalized for dehydration. Once I was released Scott drove us to our temporary living space. Housing was limited, and the military paid for us to stay in an old, bed-and-breakfast called Greylands, where we spent months waiting for a home to become available to rent.

England's sprawling green acres and small hills reminded me of Vermont. It was beautiful and rainy, and I longed to explore the vast grounds of Greylands. But the morning sickness morphed into all-day sickness, so severe that my doctor put me on anti-nausea medication. "If you don't start keeping something down, we'll need to put you back in the hospital," he warned. I took the medication, which cured the nausea, but all I wanted to do was sleep.

Eventually one of our Air Force friends got assigned base housing, and we took over his lease in a little village called Wickham Market, just weeks before our two boys were joined by a sister.

In 1994, a third son arrived, growing our family of five to a family of six during our time overseas. (I would give birth to two more daughters when we moved back to the states). Although I was pregnant or nursing and exhausted for much of our time om England, we created years of sweet memories.

We quickly made new friends and found a church. Scott and I worked in AWANA, a Christian-based children's program—and became active in the Sunday school ministry. We discovered that British amusement parks weren't all that different from their American counterparts, that Walmart was no rival for the UK's Tesco, and that car boots were something akin to flea markets or community yard sales, with Brits selling items out of the trunks—or boots, as the British called them—of their cars. We saw the guards at Buckingham Palace, photographed Big Ben, and did all manner of touristy things while also living our everyday life in a British village.

I felt wrapped in a blanket of safety, knitted together with sweet friendships, a doting husband, healthy, happy children, and a true sense of camaraderie. But in the midst of that season of sweetness stands a different kind of memory, a brief moment warning me that I would never quite measure up.

It was a crisp autumn morning, and the unexpected brightness of the sun matched my mood. I had a bounce in my step, and I eagerly dressed for church. I couldn't wait to be among friends, to watch as our kids ran around with other youngsters, and to be immersed in the preaching of God's Word. As a new Christian, I had an insatiable hunger for the Word. I always looked forward to Sunday mornings and Bible teachings, but the extra joy on that Sunday morning came from a brand-new pair of pale pink flats that I slipped my feet into. The sleek leather shoes were the first pair I had bought, aside from tennis shoes and flip-flops, since high school, and I adored them.

Later that afternoon, when the service was over, Scott and I stood in the foyer, chatting with friends. Next to us, I overheard someone compliment the pastor's wife on her new rust-colored suit. "Thank you." She accepted the compliment with a little dismissive wave. "It's definitely time to bring out the fall wardrobe. I find pastels to be so tacky at this time of year."

I froze and glanced down at my feet. I could feel the warmth spread through my body as I snuck furtive glances around to see if anyone had noticed my shoes. My pastel-colored shoes. At that moment, I time-warped back to the run-down apartment with nicotine-stained walls, and the little girl whose insides were imbued with such a deep shade of shame that it still seeped through to the outer layers, still colored my face red. *How stupid could I be?* I wondered. *Any normal person would know you don't wear pastels at this time of year. No wonder the shoes were on sale.*

I didn't own "a wardrobe," and I would never fit in with wardrobe kind of people. I was still the same hand-me-downs kind of girl who got excited over new pink flats that she bought on sale in August.

Today, decades later, I would march right past that pastor's wife, proud of my new flats, and not allow any opinion to steal my delight. Knowing that she had grown up in the south, in a different generation, I would realize she meant no harm. I would toss aside her remark as easily as peanut shells, not letting them define me. But not then.

On that fall day I told my husband I would meet him outside, snatched up our two little boys, and nearly ran to the car. As I sat there waiting, a fierce pain squeezed my heart. All kinds of feelings came sliding through like impatient toddlers on a slip 'n' slide, crashing into each other at the end of the plastic sheet. I swiped at tears and vowed that no one would ever look at me and think *tacky*. No one would view me with pity or disdain because of any lack of style. That week, I went to the library and checked out books on fashion and style. As I poured over the books, one theme echoed throughout: choose a fashion statement. I mulled it over for a while and finally decided that earrings would be my personal autograph. I would follow the clothing style of the experts, but the capstone for each outfit in my newly acquired "wardrobe" would be my earrings.

When I shopped for name brand clothing, I unwittingly added layers to the papier-mâché princess. Dressed in Liz Claiborne skirts, Saks Fifth Avenue shoes, and coordinating earrings, I was creating a girl who could smile with confidence from her pew on Sundays. But I would have to keep others at a distance, so they wouldn't realize it was just a facade.

Over time, I became enslaved to this pursuit, always searching for the unique pair of earrings that would say "I have class" or "I am somebody." Each pair would take its turn on the papier mâché princess, but not even my favorite pair, an elegant dangle of sterling silver and radiant blue topaz, could make me believe that I was anything more than a beggar.

While in England, we visited Warwick Castle, Sherwood Forest, London Zoo, and many other well-known places. We dined on fish and chips from the neighborhood fish truck on Fridays. The deep-fried fish came wrapped in paper and dripped with oil, and we devoured it while it was still hot enough to singe the roof of our mouths. We learned how to make Yorkshire Pudding, and how to thrive without a television because we were unwilling to pay the exorbitant British TV tax.

So many memories to cherish.

When my children think back to their early childhood days in England, they recall double-decker buses, a huge tarantula at the London Zoo, daunting castles with torture chambers, Robin Hood costumes complete with bows and arrows, and a knight on horseback patiently explaining each piece of his armor. They think of laughter, storybooks, and building forts.

I remember those things too.

But the memory that left the deepest imprint on my heart and soul from those years is one that I tried to leave behind when we left England. I wasn't fast enough, and it followed me back to the states. It is a memory that now symbolizes a deep testing of my faith, an initial shattering of the illusion that I could protect myself from wounds, or that I could be in control of anything by doing good works.

The memory came in the form of a letter. My heart did a little jig when I saw my name written in my husband's familiar handwriting on folded sheets of tablet paper. I loved receiving his letters and notes, and for days afterwards a silly smile would appear on my face at random moments as I reread the words in my mind.

This particular letter brought no smiles. The day it arrived began with excitement and anticipation. Scott had returned from a lengthy temporary duty assignment that afternoon. After roughhousing with the kids, unpacking his duffel bag, and gorging on fried chicken, my tired husband helped to corral the children, who more than made up for the energy we adults were lacking.

"Bedtime," Scott and I spoke in unison and laughed.

"Aww, do we have to go to bed?" five-year-old Josh protested. "We want to play with Dad!"

"There will be plenty of play time tomorrow. Dad isn't going anywhere for a while," I smiled across the room at Scott. We both sighed in relief when the last child was finally tucked in, and Scott turned out the light. We crept out of the room and stepped over the squeaky spots on the stairs on our way to tidy the living room.

"I think the travel time has caught up with me. I'm gonna head up to bed," Scott told me as he put the last toy soldier in the toybox. Before heading back up the stairs, he gave me a long, slow kiss and then handed me the letter.

Immediately, I plopped into our old gray and beige recliner that mostly hid stains from sticky toddler hands. As I began reading, my finger absently found the tiny hole in the fabric that wasn't quite visible to others. I anticipated a sweet and mushy love letter, one that would create an eagerness to follow Scott up the stairs. But the words on the paper confused me. They were a confession.

My husband had an addiction to pornography. *"It started when I was eleven years old. My friend and I found his dad's magazines. It wasn't long before I got caught up using pornography to escape many emotions that I didn't know what to do with. I thought it was something I could let go of, but I haven't been able to, especially while TDY. I have been trying to stop since we made the decision to follow Christ. I can't seem to overcome it."*

I stared at the words.

"I'm struggling and I believe the Holy Spirit is pressing me to tell you so there are no secrets between us." The letter went on to give me more details than I wanted to know. Details that crushed me.

It is easy to look back from a place of healing and see that Scott was trying to build a stronger foundation; one built on truth and transparency instead of secrets. A foundation of working together and trusting the Lord to do what only He could do.

I didn't see any of that then. Shock and hurt and anger blinded me.

Prior to our decision to live for Christ, Scott and I had both subscribed to adult magazines and viewed pornography. We had nonchalantly accepted the porn videos from my mother the first time Scott had met her because, like alcohol, it was just a part of our lives then. As a Christian, I'd had no struggle letting go of this part of my life, so I assumed Scott's inability to do the same was because of me. I told myself that obviously I wasn't enough for him to look at. Just like my mom's old boyfriend had predicted, I couldn't please a man.

In the decades since that time, science has learned a lot about addictions and how the brain works, but back then I assumed if you didn't want to do something, you just quit doing it. Since Scott couldn't "just quit," I doubted his love for me.

The perfect marriage I had proudly framed and hung in my heart had been shaken loose and lay shattered on the ground; the glass shards pressing sharply against scars from my youth. It felt like everything I had believed about my marriage had been an illusion and a lie. I couldn't see that my husband's letter was a heartfelt plea to help him become the man of God he longed to be. Instead of coming alongside him in support, thanking him for being vulnerable and open, I antagonized him. I belittled him. I accused him. I shamed and guilted him. I treated him like my enemy. I lived out the cliché that hurt people hurt people.

Because way down deep in my marrow, I was crushed. My faith was shattered. People *still* could not be trusted, not even the ones who declared their love for me. Maybe God couldn't be trusted. Or maybe I just wasn't good enough to deserve good things. I instantly stepped back into childhood beliefs and coping mechanism.

Haim Ginott, an American schoolteacher and child psychologist once said, "Children are like wet cement. Whatever falls on them makes an impression." I unwittingly lived out that truth.

In addition to the mocking words of mom's former boyfriend, I didn't realize how deeply my father's infidelity to my mother had impacted me. I didn't see I still had a crater-sized hole of mistrust.

Although Scott had not engaged in a physical affair, his confession enlarged that hole.

In the following days, I tore at him with accusations: "You are just like my father! And just like my mother's old boyfriend!" I spewed at him with enough ferocity to make him cringe. "You can't be trusted." I felt something akin to hatred towards him. Really it was a renewed loathing towards myself.

I looked in the mirror and saw each imperfection, every varicose vein, and my small, childlike build. Once again, I heard the mocking words of mom's boyfriend talking about my flat chest and telling me how men liked big- busted women and unless I developed, I couldn't please anyone.

I thought I had released all those feelings of shame and self-loathing towards my physical body that had sprouted up from that man's constant degrading words. But now the old fears and shame came roaring back in like a tidal wave washing away my newfound feelings of safety and trust. I was sure Scott's need to look at other women was because I was flawed. I was less than. I was defective.

I no longer believed Scott when he told me I was beautiful. Doubts rose when he said, "I love you."

The night I read Scott's confession, I barely slept. I tossed and turned, and when I finally fell into a fitful sleep, I dreamed about a flowered dress from my childhood. It had been a lovely dress with tiny yellow flowers and a full, billowing skirt. It wasn't mine, though. I had borrowed it from my friend Sonya to wear to an elementary school dance. When I put the dress on, I became somebody new.

I closed my eyes and spun around my bedroom and, as I did, promises twirled with the skirt until they settled like the soft, cool, material against my skin, soothing and hopeful. I was somebody new. No longer a welfare kid. No longer a broken girl whose insides were stained a tenebrous shade of shame. No longer a frightened adolescent who had to lull herself to sleep each night, dreaming of the prince who would turn the ugly stepchild into a beloved princess. Instead, I was beautiful. Clean. Castle-worthy.

But looking around my childhood room, I was reminded that life is rarely a fairy tale and that I had been foolish to think I could be Cinderella. The nicotine-stained ceiling of our house remained an ugly brownish-yellow and no magic wand poofed the mismatched Tupperware into fine Royal Doulton. The mice that scratched and chewed behind the apartment walls never transformed into powerful horses but remained mute rodents that continued to gnaw at my tenuous hold on hope.

And my soul? My soul remained in tattered hand-me-downs. Because in the end, it was just a borrowed dress with tiny yellow flowers and a full billowing skirt. When the elementary school dance was over, and the paper streamers were yanked down by giddy adolescents, I returned home. Slowly, I pulled the flowered dress over my head. It dropped into a shapeless heap at my feet. The next day, I dutifully returned the dress to my friend, its rightful owner. Then I sat on the dilapidated front porch and waited for the glass slipper that never arrived.

Until Scott.

When I met Scott in 1987, it felt like he slid that princess shoe right over my deformed toes, transforming me. He was handsome and popular and well respected. With him, I had a new last name. A new identity. And *if someone like that loved me, then I must be castle-worthy*, I assured myself.

The day we stood before a justice of the peace, I had already sewn his last name on my military uniforms, eager to trade in my old identity as fast as I could. I was once again the girl in the flowered dress with the full, billowing skirt. Loved. Cherished. Transformed. *Except this time*, I thought, *the dress is mine to keep.*

I believed it, until Scott's letter. If my husband could keep his pornography addiction a secret, what else wasn't he telling me? Could I believe anything he said? Did that mean I was still a nobody?

The trouble with merely putting a new label over an old belief is that it doesn't really change what is beneath. And the trouble with allowing someone else to define us is that other people are flawed too. If I wrap my identity in a new title or another mortal, I will find that the shiny new facade eventually becomes threadbare and frayed. I learned this as the lovely new dress I had been hiding beneath became tattered, stained, and bedraggled. I was shocked to discover that underneath I was grimier than ever. I found myself once again searching for a new identity, chasing after another garment that seemed just out of my price range. In her memoir *Thin Places,* Mary E. Duluth shares her lifelong struggle with shame mongering. She says that it was so tightly woven into her fibers that only God could free her from it.

I can relate, Mary. I can relate, I thought as I read her words.

In the season following Scott's confession, I again felt shame so deeply embedded in my heart and mind that I thought I would never escape, that nothing I had done or could ever do would emancipate me. It was the same emotional shackling I had felt in my teenage years. In fact, when I was eighteen, I wrote the following poem as I attempted to leave my past behind by joining the Air Force:

Vernal House of the Old

*A broken television set
and confused dreams
are all that's left of this house.
Stained wallpaper
draws diagrams of desolation
against a chalkboard of hope.
It tells me to run to tomorrow.
But this house dwells in me.
Will I ever be able to leave?
I packed my clothes years ago,
The windows have all been locked.
Memories are stored
beside broken Barbie Dolls
and skinned knees.
It seems the time is here.
Yet I ask
Will I ever leave?*

9: Maintaining the Illusion

EVEN THEN I KNEW.

I knew.

I knew that no matter where I went, no matter what goals I achieved, what awards or honors I received, or how many charities I gave to, I could never escape the essence of who I was and where I had been. The promises of the flowered dress would never really belong to me. My husband's letter and the confession of a pornography addiction he couldn't overcome proved it.

I didn't need a new last name or a new dress. I needed to be made new. And I was. I knew in my head that when I gave my life to Christ, He promised to make all things new. But I couldn't embrace that truth because I was too busy trying to reinvent myself, so that no one would recognize me as a clumsy, uneducated, underdeveloped, welfare kid. I didn't want anyone to catch even a glimpse of the drunk I had been in my earlier years. I had hidden the truth of my home life as an adolescent. And now, I would hide my knowledge of Scott's addiction too.

I was more determined than ever to control my image and my life. Sure, I knew I had been made new by God's gift of grace, but instead of simply accepting that freedom, I was determined to earn it by making myself worthy.

I became Suzie Homemaker. I taught myself to make homemade bread and strawberry jam, and I learned how to keep a spotless house. I went to church whenever a service took place and invited people to our home afterwards. I put a weight bench and stationary bike in our oversized bedroom and exercised daily. I constantly worked to create the person I wanted to be.

I wanted that magical dress that would transform me. Even if I made it out of papier-mâché.

I would use my family, friends, and church to help me add the delicate layers I needed to create the illusion of that new dress. It was not the church's fault, but for wounded people, *doing* church as opposed to *being* the church usually stems from a wrong motive. Church can be a place to make ourselves feel better if we measure ourselves by the old covenant which is law-based, instead of by the Messiah Himself.

In the past I had used alcohol and relationships to hide my deeply buried need for love, identity, and worth. Once I surrendered to Christ, I was a new person, but the new me still looked in the old mirror to check my appearance, to get assurance and validation, to be in control of how others saw me.

I devoured Scriptures and they were a feast for this emaciated actress. I learned biblical truths that amazed me. But I took them in as head knowledge, following the "rules," believing that doing so would make me worthy of His love. The staggering, unearnable, freely given grace described in His Word didn't reach into the dark, secret rooms of my heart because I never opened the door and let His healing light wash over my feelings of shame and hurt. I thought I had to apply the principles myself, in my own strength.

I tried, but I couldn't do it.

Trying to live out the Scriptures apart from the Holy Spirit is merely an attempt at behavior modification. The vicious "I'm gonna," "I need to," "I should," "I must" cycle is exhausting. It wore me out.

I tried to convince myself that my past was behind me, and that any stains would eventually disappear if I dumped a bottle of good deeds on them and applied enough elbow grease. A constant niggling told me that I needed to scrub and scrub, the way my mother sometimes got down on her hands and knees after a particularly rough weekend of drinking and stripped yellowed wax from our old linoleum floor until her hands were raw and her knees red. The way Cinderella scrubbed her stepmother's house before magic and a glass slipper transformed her.

My scrub brush was ministry. Scott and I served every Sunday in the Children's ministry and continued serving in AWANA. I taught Bible studies and started a homeschool support group for moms. Every time someone thanked me or sent an e-mail or greeting card telling me that I had inspired or encouraged them, I mentally nailed it to my "I Now Have Value" wall of certificates.

I knew the truth, though.

These women were seeing a mask of service and head knowledge. In reality, I was nothing more than a papier mâché princess, dangling precariously. I was haunted by the gnawing fear that with the slightest whisper of wind, the string—and the facade—would break. The papier mâché princess would split open, revealing the irony. There were no prizes inside. I was still empty.

So I held most people at arm's length, letting them get just close enough to see the glass slipper, the long white gloves, the Cinderella dress. But I didn't let them close enough to see it was merely a hardened, empty shell of glue and tissue paper.

The *act* of ministry or service couldn't clean anything, but it was my newest flavor of alcohol. I had unwittingly exchanged one illusion of control for another, more acceptable one.

Ministry for the right reasons, with the Spirit's power, is a God-thing. But ministry to create a new and improved version of self is like grasping at the wind. And when things are kept in the dark, when we bury or ignore hurts and lies and sins, there is no moving forward or prospering.

There is only death. It is in the light—in carrying secrets and deceptions into truth's authority—that grace and mercy can begin breathing new life to the dying.

I didn't know that then. I served, and I hid the wounds of my husband's pornography addiction from my friends, sometimes even from myself because it was like a huge, ugly stain on my new princess dress. But hiding things doesn't make them disappear.

So those wounds–the monster I tried to lock in the back of the closet–eventually began banging on the door and growling loudly enough that others could hear. Even with my fingers shoved in my ears *I* could hear it.

Shame elbowed its way back in, and it dragged rage with it.

I thought when I became a Christ follower, I had gotten rid of anger, but I had merely packed it into a box, scribbled The Past on the top flap, and shoved it on a shelf in my closet. Before long, I had forgotten about it. Now new feelings of inferiority tipped that box over and moldy bitterness towards men in my childhood spilled out over everything. That bitterness grew and festered, and Scott became the main target.

My anger was always there, silent and smoldering. It lurked beneath dual banners—an old white flag of shame and defeat and my newer, brightly colored banner of perfectionism.

This anger affected all areas of my life. It showed up in the way I parented. I held my children to extremely high standards and yelled when they didn't clean their messes or didn't obey. Anger affected my daily expectations of myself. I created unrealistic to-do lists and berated myself when I didn't check off every last item. It stunted my spiritual growth because I felt bitter towards God. I felt that He loved others more than He loved me.

Mostly anger affected my marriage, nearly destroying the one human relationship that mattered the most to me. The trust I had in men to be faithful husbands had been a worn strand to begin with and discovering Scott had kept secrets from me frayed it even more. Resorting to my old protective method of hurt or be hurt, I demeaned and accused Scott. I sliced him with my words. I erected an emotional wall that left both of us feeling alone.

Stuck in the miry clay of my own addiction to control and to protect myself, I searched for self-help programs. But it didn't matter if I climbed twelve steps or ninety-nine, when I got to the top, I would find myself staring back down at the same chains.

I could see the old Marie rising up to take charge. I didn't want that but didn't know how to fix anything. Scott and I approached pastors for counsel. I read books on managing anger. I studied the Scriptures. I spent hours upon hours in the Word. All of these things led to a measure of success, but at best, I was managing anger and experiencing behavior modification.

I could mostly *control* my anger but not the host of internal emotions, the fears and anxiety, that kept me awake at night. I thought controlling my behaviors was as good as it was going to get. I couldn't free myself from the destructive emotions. I couldn't heal Scott's addiction. And I certainly couldn't share the struggle I was going through with anyone.

I considered divorce, because I didn't know if a marriage that had once harbored secrets could survive. Under my control, it probably wouldn't have. But handing the reins to God—my first lesson in letting go—changed everything.

PART FOUR:

LOOSENING MY GRIP

The Mirror Revisited (2002)

Cell-like bathroom
Dime store mirror
Stifling steam dissipating
A figure emerges
Scarecrow's head, body of tin, lion's tale lying
Dorothy's longing snatched
From the towel rack
Rubbed briskly
Chafing the skin
A rush to get dressed
Bathroom door opened
From a gentle breeze
Calling quietly
No ruby slippers but
Take another look
Cell-like bathroom
Dime store mirror
Stifling steam dissipating
A figure emerges
Eagle's wings, heart of flesh, dead bones dancing

10: Can These Bones Live?

A SLIGHT, PERSISTENT SHAKING OF MY PILLOW PULLED ME from a deep sleep.

"Mommy, Mommy, it's snowding! It's snowding!"

I forced my eyes open, and my three-year-old daughter's face came into focus.

"Come see, come see!" she said, tugging at my hand.

I smiled at the way she repeated everything she said. I glanced at the alarm clock, and the two-inch red numbers stared back: 7:03 a.m. My smile disappeared. I had overslept.

Again.

I struggled to get out of bed most mornings. I no longer woke up refreshed but physically and emotionally exhausted from the mental battles I fought every night.

It used to be that I would fall asleep right away, nestled in Scott's arms and wake up long before the children were out of bed. These nights, I turned my back to my husband, moved to the far edge of the bed, and I wrapped myself in bitter thoughts instead of his arms. The thoughts were relentless echoes from my adolescent years: *You idiot, did you really believe he is attracted to you? With your childlike figure? You will never measure up to those women in Playboy, with their perfect, photoshopped bodies. Don't believe him when he says this addiction is not about you. You'll always look like a child, not a real woman. It's all about you and your defects.*

This morning was no different. I was drained. Still, Michelle's impatience and excitement persuaded me to throw off the comforter and get moving. I pulled on my faded bathrobe and followed my daughter into the living room where her siblings had pushed aside the vertical blinds and pressed their noses against the cold glass of our sliding door. Overnight the brown, barren backyard had transformed into a glistening white blanket, as breathtaking as a newborn's first cry. Large, white flakes continued to fall, and the children clamored to go outside to play.

"Not yet," I said. "You can go outside after breakfast when it warms up a smidge." I poured myself a cup of hazelnut coffee and shooed the kids off to get dressed while I sliced oranges and set boxes of cereal–Honey Nut Cheerios, Cinnamon Toast Crunch, and Kix–on the table. I grabbed five bowls, then dumped a few Cheerios on the tray of the baby's highchair.

While the kids wolfed down their cereal and slurped the milk from their bowls, I dug through the coat closet and carried a colorful pile of boots, snow pants, mittens, hats, and coats to the living room. I dumped them in a heap by the sliding doors and looked out at the blinding snow. The sun's rays hit the top layer of tiny snow crystals, making it look like spilled glitter. I marveled at how quickly the desolate-looking landscape from yesterday had turned into such a place of mesmerizing beauty. Overnight, the dead grass, armless G.I. Joes, and rusty Hot Wheels were buried beneath a pristine white covering. I wished it was that easy to transform the dry, hard, and broken places in my heart.

Lord, my heart feels so dead towards Scott and our marriage, my spirit cried. I still loved my husband, yet the anger I felt towards him combined with the loathing of myself were strangling the life out of the good feelings. A familiar Scripture stepped into my thoughts: "Come now, and let us reason together, saith the Lord: though your sins be as scarlet, they shall be as white as snow; though they be red like crimson, they shall be as wool" (Isaiah 1:18 KJV).

"Mommy, we're dressed!" the kids' voices rose above the quietness of God's spirit within me. "Can we go outside now? Can we?"

I zipped jackets, tucked in mittens and scarves, and finally closed the door behind what looked like five colorful penguins waddling out to the back yard. I remained in front of the glass door, watching the kids play. Matthew and Josh tossed snowballs while Kyle rolled snow into a lopsided body for a snowman. Alyssa threw herself onto her back and flapped her arms and legs, then struggled to her feet to view her tiny angel imprint. Michelle laughed at all the antics. Elizabeth giggled from the playpen I had set in front of the glass doors.

I marveled at their energy and pure joy. I had neither this morning. *Lord, please let Your grace fall like snow upon my heart,* I pleaded.

Come now, and let us reason together. The words from Scripture repeated themselves over and over in my heart, until I realized God's spirit was responding to my cries. I poured another cup of hazelnut coffee and slumped onto the couch. I tentatively opened my Bible, knowing intuitively that God had a specific word for me that morning. I landed in Ezekiel 37, an unfamiliar passage to me. I read through the beginning of the chapter, and it is difficult to put into words what God did in that moment. He spoke so clearly, so directly to my heart and to my needs, that I knew I would never be the same.

There are countless times when I have heard a word from God through a preacher or at a Bible study or from a book, and I have been deeply moved. I have been changed by the message, or at least motivated to change. But the times when God has spoken directly into my heart are incomparable. The changes that take place inwardly in these moments have sometimes been so powerful that I literally break out into dance moves because I can't contain the joy. Other times His words to me are like being seared with a branding iron: painful but permanently marking me as His. This was one of those times.

The night before, when I tossed and turned, thinking about Scott's struggles with pornography and how trust had been broken when he hid his addiction from me, I contemplated divorce. *Could we afford it? Could I possibly bear shared custody? What kind of job could I get after being a stay-at-home mom for the past decade? What would my church family think?*

While reading through Ezekiel 37 that morning, all my questions about figuring out the details of a divorce drifted away like balloons released from a child's grip, disappearing until they were mere specks in a vast sky of faith.

"Can these bones live?" the Spirit of the LORD had asked Ezekiel as He led him through a valley filled with dry, lifeless bones. Ezekiel, a man of great faith and obedience, replied: "Sovereign LORD, you alone know."

The chapter goes on to depict the amazing story of Ezekiel obediently prophesying to that valley of dead, dried up bones, telling them that they were going to live. And they did. God put sinew and flesh and skin upon the bones and then He breathed new life into them. These dead bones rose up and became a great army, a force of confidence and strength. It was a picture of a hopeless nation being brought back to life by the power of God. From death to life. From impossibility to joyful expectation. From defeat to victory.

As I imagined the great rattling of the bones coming together, I felt a rattling of my own, a rattling in my very core.

Marie, can this marriage flourish? The question from the Spirit pierced me like a physical shock. Could it? Could my marriage not just survive but flourish? It appeared hopeless to me. I had been trying to fix it myself, to bring the joy back to life, but I couldn't.

Sovereign Lord, You alone know. It seems impossible to me, my heart cried.

Child, nothing is impossible for Me. Give it to Me. The anger, the expectations, the fears, the wounds. I am Healer. You are not.

I believed. Deep in my spirit, I believed. Something shifted and like a bird escaping its cage, soaring into freedom was released from me. I didn't have to figure this out. I didn't have to fix anyone. I didn't have to control anything. This wasn't a pastor or a friend giving me advice. This was God speaking into my heart, and I responded with my mustard-seed-size faith. *Lord, I believe. Help my unbelief. I give my marriage to You.*

If life were a television show, this is where I would cue the "happily ever after" music. But this was real life. And the life that Ezekiel prophesied into those dead bones occurred through a process—bones rattling back together, then sinew and flesh and skin covering the bones, and finally God breathing into them before they stood on their feet and became a mighty army. So it would be with my marriage.

That night, instead of moving away from Scott when I slid beneath the heavy comforter, I folded into him. Inhaling the familiar scent of Irish Spring soap, feeling his rough, mechanic-skinned fingers running up and down my arms, my soul exhaled. My run-away heart was home.

When I handed control to God, I had no idea *how* things would turn out. But I knew that in His hands was where I wanted my future to be. I had already seen what He had done with the parts of my life I had handed over to Him, and I wanted more of that. More peace. More joy.

God is faithful.

Spoiler alert: thirty-five years later, my husband is my very best friend, confidante, lover, encourager, emotional supporter, and provider. I cannot fathom life without him.

It has been a process. Finger by finger the Lord pried away of my grip on the illusion that I could control anything other than myself. And it began the day that I let the breath of God take control of my marriage rather than letting insecurities, childhood wounds, and my own protective ideas run the show. I also want to be very clear: this was a word God spoke to *me* personally about *my* marriage. There has never been abuse, or physical infidelity in our relationship—just a trunk full of addictions, lies we believed about ourselves, and wounds that we needed to sort through. Apart from God's grace, I suspect we would have kept carrying all those heavy burdens until we collapsed. We would have quit on us.

Replacing control with trusting God with my marriage was just the beginning. Much like a living Whack-a-Mole game, the need to control continued to pop up in other areas in my life: my children, my children's health, my health, job security. I couldn't force the outcomes I wanted from any of it.

Long before I met Scott, my life had been about fighting to control my pain, my own addictions, and my image. Now I had children. And the desire to control expanded. As a mom, I felt an overwhelming responsibility to protect and shield my kids. I confused my responsibility—and my personal *ability*—with God's. I wanted to give my kids a carefree childhood, free from gnawing worries and a volatile environment. I was determined that they would never have to battle with the things that children from broken homes often come up against: shame, poverty, uncertainty, and worry.

But those aren't the only battles that a child can face. Pain can step into even the healthiest of families. And sometimes parents discover they are powerless to do anything about it.

"Mom, what's for supper? I'm starving!" Josh asked. At fifteen, he was usually hungrier than he had been as a newborn. And crankier. He rolled his eyes when I responded with a chipper "Peanut butter sandwiches and beans!"

"Peanut butter again?" eleven-year-old Alyssa chimed in. "I wish I lived next door with Johnny. Last night he got two whole hamburgers for dinner."

My daughter didn't really want to move next door, and actually we were having lasagna for dinner. Alyssa and I were practicing our lines for an upcoming Christmas play that our church was performing. My family—except for our youngest daughter Elizabeth who was just five—had been cast as the main characters. I had not taken part in theater since my early Air Force days and forgot how much I loved acting. I loved this new experience of doing a play as a family, learning our lines, finding costumes and props, and getting up on stage to practice together.

The only cloud during that time was Elizabeth's ongoing battle with headaches and what seemed to be an eye infection. In early December she had what we thought was a bout of the flu followed by a swollen eyelid and redness in her eye, but there was no accompanying discharge that would indicate pinkeye. Dr. Headley, her pediatrician conferred with another doctor, and they prescribed an antibiotic. The swelling went down, but the headaches persisted. Initially, Elizabeth tagged along with us when we went to rehearsals. She played with other kids from the church while the rest of the family practiced *The Richest Family in Town*.

The week before Christmas, Elizabeth's headaches became severe enough that she couldn't tolerate noise or bright lights. She stayed with our friend Steve during the final rehearsals leading up to the Christmas production. I fretted about leaving her but didn't know what else to do.

The play was a hit, and my still-longing-to-be-worthy ego loved moving the audience to tears while in character. The exuberance carried over into Christmas and the following days. But on December 29, Elizabeth's eyelid once again swelled up. I called her pediatrician.

"I'm going to prescribe an antibiotic again. I'm probably being overly cautious, but let's schedule a CT scan to make sure nothing else is going on," Dr. Headly told me. I heard her clicking away on her computer. "The hospital will call you with details, but I have her scheduled at Children's hospital for tomorrow afternoon."

The speed of the CT scan appointment surprised me, and I got the sense that the doctor was more concerned than she was letting on. I didn't like city driving—especially in downtown Denver—so both Scott and I went to the appointment for Elizabeth. She was happy-go-lucky on the drive, and her attention vacillated between a new stuffed animal and looking for houses with Christmas wreaths on their doors. There was no foreshadowing of what her future held. She looked adorable in the new pink jeans and the matching sweater she had received from my stepmom for Christmas. Her hair hung down to her waist, and she reminded me of a little pixie.

We didn't have to wait long once we arrived at the cheerful, kid-focused hospital in Denver. Elizabeth was soon positioned on a table, her hair moved aside so the massive machine could take images of her head. She chatted with the technician, answering questions about her age, her favorite new stuffed animal, and what she ate for lunch.

The test itself was completed in seconds. "If you wait here, we'll be back with the results soon," the technician told us.

Soon apparently was an ambiguous term, and it was nearly an hour before a different technician returned. "We are going to try this again, but this time we are going to use a special dye so that we can see better. Is that okay with you, Elizabeth?" The technician directed her question to Elizabeth, while looking at us for confirmation. We nodded.

"Okay," Elizabeth agreed, not really understanding. Moments later, her happy-go-lucky nature disappeared, and her big brown eyes filled with tears when the technician inserted a needle in her hand. I hated seeing my daughter hurt, and I mentally willed the second scan to be quick.

It was but then came more waiting. Finally, the technician returned. "Mr. and Mrs. Isom, we have Dr. Headley on the phone. She is going to explain the results to you," the technician said and led us to a nearby telephone. Something was off. I grabbed the receiver.

"Well, there is no infection," the doctor told me.

"Hurray!" I responded, but the pediatrician wasn't finished.

"They did find a mass behind Elizabeth's eye. Someone from oncology will be down to speak with you soon. I know this is overwhelming. Please keep me informed."

It took a few seconds for her words to register. *Oncology? Wasn't that the cancer unit? What did they have to do with eye infections?* I handed the receiver back to the technician who was looking at me with pity.

"Someone from oncology will be with you shortly," she confirmed Dr. Headley's words. Scott looked at me, questions written all over his face.

"They found a mass?" I said, but it was more a question than a statement. I repeated the rest of the words I'd just heard to my husband and tears filled my eyes. Elizabeth was engaged in an animated conversation with her stuffed animal, completely oblivious to the talks going on around her.

Moments later, an oncologist arrived. "I'm Dr. Albano," she said. Her demeanor bordered on brusque as she shook mine and Scott's hands before ushering us into a small room. "Let me show you the scans, and we can talk."

She pointed to a set of four large films, each depicting different views of Elizabeth's skull. She tapped on one area and explained, "This is the mass we are referring to. It is located directly behind her right eye. We will need to do an MRI tomorrow so that we can better assess the situation and come up with a plan of treatment. We don't usually do surgical removal of tumors in children but treat them with chemotherapy and radiation."

Chemotherapy? Radiation? I had not yet wrapped my head around the word *cancer*, and now the oncologist was throwing more hideous words at us. I wanted to grab the words and throw them back at her, tell her she made a mistake. Those words were not for us, not for the sweet little girl in a pink sweater with hair down to her waist, chatting excitedly to her Care Bear.

No matter how fiercely I tried to will it away, to pray it away, an MRI was scheduled for the following morning. On the way home, Scott and I rode silently while Elizabeth filled the quiet with her little sing-song voice chattering nonstop.

That night, our pastor, his wife, and our close friends the Petries came over to pray with us. Reality set in when I opened my eyes and saw tears streaming down the faces of three grown men. Radiation and chemotherapy were in our daughter's immediate future. *We could lose this precious child.* I didn't allow myself to dwell on that thought and shoved a box of tissues across the table to Scott.

Early the next morning, I brushed Elizabeth's hair, and weaved it into two long braids. With a splattering of freckles across her porcelain-colored skin, she looked like one of the ceramic dolls that Scott's mom made. "We are going back to the hospital today," I told her with a feigned brightness in my voice.

"Yay! I love the Mouse House!" Elizabeth shouted, referring to a large doll house inside a glass display case at the children's hospital.

"Sweetie, the doctors need to do more tests, kind of like yesterday. Daddy and I will be there the whole time," I assured her.

But it was my five-year-old who would end up comforting me, with her spirited countenance and easy-going nature despite all the hovering doctors, the needles, the endless waiting.

"It's okay, Mommy."

The MRI confirmed Dr. Albano's fears. "It appears to be a malignant, aggressive form of bone cancer," she told us. She pointed to an image. "The bone is completely shattered here. We originally planned to do a craniotomy to biopsy the tumor, but I spoke with an orbital surgeon here at the hospital." She faced us. "Dr. Durairaj believes he can go behind the eye socket with a needle to draw tissue. It's much less invasive than removing a piece of Elizabeth's skull. I will introduce you to him and you can decide which option you think is best."

When I first met Dr. Vik Durairaj I wanted to shout *NO!* We shook hands, and his enormous one swallowed mine. *There is no way a hand that size can perform the delicate procedure that Dr. Albano described to us,* I thought. But this still seemed like the best option. We gave Dr. Durairaj the go-ahead to draw tissue from behind Elizabeth's eye and signed the necessary paperwork. The biopsy was scheduled for January 2, just two days away. We returned home with Elizabeth to wait.

It felt like another finger being pried from my death grip on the illusion of being in control.

The afternoon before the surgery, I wrote these words in my journal:

> *Lord, how can it be? How can our beautiful, funny, endlessly curious Elizabeth have a tumor? A cancerous tumor. I keep thinking this isn't really happening. Please, LORD, help Elizabeth to be strong tomorrow, to get through this. My heart is shattered at the thought of losing her. Lord, You have given us the gift of Elizabeth – You have created her and ultimately she is in Your hands not mine. But still I cry out, asking that You listen to the weeping of Your people, and allow us to keep our precious girl, allow her to live a long and full life.*

That evening, my friend Marci came over to pray with me. We ended our prayers with a teary Amen and an inexplicable peace covered me. I released the sadness and unknowns to God and experienced a subtle yet pivotal shift from fear and grief to trust. I still knew I could not force the outcome I wanted from the biopsy. The reality that cancer could take our daughter still took my breath away, made my chest ache. The what ifs still clung heavy, like wet wool. But each time I felt the weight of fear, I placed myself under the truth that I knew: *God is good. God is trustworthy.*

I cried out for strength, and He gave it. I asked for my moments of unbelief to be transformed into faith. A Scripture began running through my mind, and I repeated the words over and over, sometimes silently, sometimes out loud: "To bestow on them a crown of beauty instead of ashes, the oil of joy instead of mourning, and a garment of praise instead of a spirit of despair" (Isaiah 61:3 NIV).

I already understood the spirit of despair. It chased after me much of my life, including when we first received the news of Elizabeth's tumor. What I didn't know was how soon I would find myself wrapped snugly in the mantle of praise and thanksgiving.

The following morning, we tiptoed into the girls' bedroom to wake Elizabeth, trying not to disturb her older sisters. But they, too, were instantly awake. They hugged Elizabeth with a ferocity that made me cry. No one wanted breakfast, so Scott, Elizabeth and I headed to the hospital before the sun even opened its eyes. As we drove, it felt like time was moving at a sloth's pace, like we were in a slow-motion film, but everything sped up once we arrived at the hospital. We met with doctors and signed more forms. We helped Elizabeth into a hospital gown that looked ridiculously large on her tiny frame. The doctors allowed Scott to lift her onto the hospital gurney, and I held tightly to her hand.

"We are going to put a mask on your face and have you breathe in some sleep medicine while counting to ten. Can you count to ten?" an anesthesiologist asked. She smiled when Elizabeth nodded emphatically. The doctor then showed her a clear egg-shaped plastic mask with a blue ring. "Let's try it for practice, okay?"

Elizabeth nodded. The doctor placed the mask briefly over her mouth and nose and then continued talking to her. "You can choose what flavor medicine you want. I have bubblegum and grape and cherry and—"

"Bubblegum." Elizabeth's voice quivered and she swiped at tears, doing her best to look brave. I looked away so she couldn't see me wipe my own tears away.

The anesthesiologist fiddled with something and then again put the mask on our daughter. "One. Two. Three." Before she got to four, Elizabeth was out. I didn't want to leave her side. I wanted to scream and chase after the doctors who were wheeling my little girl away from me. My knees buckled. Scott held me up. I wondered how I would make it through the hour-long surgery.

"Let me show you where you can wait," a voice broke through the surrealness, and someone led us to a brightly lit room.

What a stupid color, I thought as I looked at a yellow wall. It seemed incompatible with the somber group of statue-like parents waiting for their children to come out of surgery. I verbalized the thought to Scott, but he had a different perspective.

"Yellow is a color of hope."

Scott's dad and stepmom arrived to wait with us, and after a brief exchange of hugs, we sat immobile and silent like the others in the room. The next hour felt like a day, the long minutes interrupted only by smiling doctors who arrived to lead grateful parents back to recovery rooms. I tried to read but couldn't focus. I kept watching the hallway for Dr. Vik's looming figure. Another half hour passed, more doctors arrived, more parents left, and yet there was no sign of the orbital surgeon whose large hands were going to draw tissue from behind Elizabeth's tiny eye socket. Finally, I went to the information desk.

"Our daughter Elizabeth Isom was supposed to be done with surgery an hour ago. Do you know what is taking so long?" I asked.

The receptionists picked up a phone and pushed a button. She turned away from me and I couldn't hear the conversation. When she turned back, her demeanor had shifted slightly. "Just hang on. It's taking a little longer than expected."

Duh, I KNOW that. My sarcastic thoughts shocked me, until my stomach growled its own frustration, and I realized I was starving, which only added to the onslaught of emotions. But food would have to wait.

Two hours and fifteen minutes.

Two hours and thirty minutes.

Two hours and forty-five minutes.

I sat quietly, but inside I was a screaming mess, wondering what was taking so long, wanting to go shake the receptionist and get answers. Finally, more than three hours after they had wheeled Elizabeth away, I looked up and saw Dr. Vik shuffling towards us. Unlike the other doctors, he was not smiling. Instead, he was shaking his head, looking dazed. My heart did the proverbial leap out of my chest. Part of me wanted to shout at him to hurry up and another part wanted him to stop, to not say what I knew he was going to say.

"Sorry it took so long," he said when he finally stood before us, "but we were pleasantly surprised."

Pleasantly surprised? Dr. Vik's unexpected words washed over me, and I slumped against Scott as the doctor explained.

"Elizabeth has something called Eosinophilic Granuloma, a form of Langerhans Cell Histiocytosis." The words flowed out of his mouth before I could understand them, much less pronounce them.

"What does that mean?" Esther, my stepmom, asked while I was still trying to process what Dr. Vik had said.

"It's not cancer."

"Praise the Lord!" Esther, Scott, and I exclaimed at the same time, causing others in the room to glance our way. My face flushed, but I quickly forgot about the other parents.

"I went in there pretty certain of what I would find," Dr. Vik admitted, "and given the images of her shattered bone, it was a bleak outlook. Instead, what we discovered is that she has a very treatable disease." I exhaled and the surgeon continued. "We were fortunate because we have someone in our lab who is familiar with Langerhans Cell Histiocytosis."

"What do you mean?" Scott asked.

"Langerhans Cell Histiocytosis is an orphan disease. It is extremely rare and not much research has been done on it. We could have missed it." Dr. Vik gave us a moment to digest his words before leading us back to Elizabeth's recovery room.

Elizabeth was just waking up. Groggy and disoriented, she grabbed at a large white bandage that covered her eye. "Ow, ow, ow. I can't see." Her voice rose in panic until Scott reached her side and found her hand.

"Hey, we are here now. You did great." His words quieted her, but she was soon whimpering in pain again.

"Her eye was scratched during surgery. It will hurt for a bit but should heal quickly," a nurse told us. "She'll need to stay here for a couple of hours, and then you can take her home."

Dr. Albano entered the room. "Hey, Elizabeth, you did great! Such a brave girl," she told Elizabeth before turning to us. "We will be starting her on steroids and then she will need to begin chemotherapy. Even though this is not cancer, it is still treated in a similar way. Most likely she will need radiation as well. I know it sounds scary, but we are very, very thankful that we did not find bone cancer."

For the next month, Elizabeth took what she dubbed her "happy pills." By the time the swelling and bruises from surgery finally faded from her eye, the steroids had turned our daughter into a chubby, shiny-cheeked little girl. We cut about fourteen inches off her wavy brown hair when it became a hassle with the frequent CT scans and oncology visits.

Three months later, when we celebrated her sixth birthday, she looked like an entirely different child, but the steroids were so effective that she was able to have chemo treatment in the form of pills rather than needing a port surgically placed. And then the chemo was so effective that Dr. Albano decided that radiation was not needed.

Friends and church members inundated us with meals, cards, prayers, gifts, and financial support during this time. Elizabeth's room became a colorful zoo for the dozens and dozens of stuffed animals that friends, family, and strangers sent. Every need was met. It could have turned out differently. Rather than years of follow up oncology visits, we could have buried our youngest daughter. We could have been left with a hole in our "Isom 8" nickname. We were surely blessed in countless ways. Perhaps one of the greatest blessings for me during that season was not a tangible one. It was letting go of the belief that I was in control of my children's health. Letting go of the belief that if I made sure that they ate right, took vitamins, got plenty of sleep, played outdoors, had regular doctors' visits, and brushed their teeth, all would be well. Letting go of the formula. Letting go of the belief that I was solely responsible. And as I released all these beliefs, it freed me of the heavy weight of anxiety I had been lugging around. It was a traumatic and yet freeing season as I once again loosened my grip on control. I learned that no matter what happened, God would carry me through.

After that, it should have been an easy transition to let go in other areas, to realize that while I can make choices on how to raise my children, ultimately I am not in control of the choices *they* make.

I was a slow learner, though, and it took many more lessons before the truth that I am not in control became permanently etched on my heart.

11: A Cry from Detox

FOR SEVENTEEN YEARS, SCOTT AND I RAISED OUR CHILDREN in an alcohol-free home. But that is not how we started.

At first, the idea of *not* drinking had been a fleeting thought landing briefly like a butterfly after we had just used our gas credit card to buy beer. Or spent too much of our tight budget on liquor and didn't have enough money left to take Kyle and Josh to the zoo. *Maybe we should just quit drinking.* I'd always brushed the thought away.

Then one weekend the truth that hit was more painful than the throbbing headache keeping me in bed. *You are creating the same life for your children that you hated when you were growing up. Maybe you don't have strangers crashing on the couch, but you are still spending all your extra money on alcohol, still waking up with such a hangover that your children are forced to be quiet, still wasting days of sunshine because you are sick. Is that really the life you want?*

It had been, quite literally, a sobering thought. I *didn't* want to raise my kids that way. And I *didn't* want to pass the poison-filled baton of addiction to my kids. I wanted to be more like my neighbor, Felicia, who didn't drink and was always so full of energy and life.

Scott and I made a commitment to quit drinking. It was excruciating at first, and we yo-yoed for a while. Or rather *I* yo-yoed for a while. "Hey, let's get a six-pack tonight," I often said to Scott. "We've done so well and drinking once in a while doesn't hurt."

I soon became Delilah to Scott's Samson, convincing him—after weeks of not drinking—that a few beers would be okay. Or I would assure my husband that I was going to "just have one" when we hung out with our drinking buddies. But I rarely stopped at one and would wake up with a throbbing head and a heart filled with regret.

After we surrendered our lives to the Lord, the yo-yoing stopped. We made a lot of new friends who didn't need the influence of alcohol on picnics, trips to the beach, or over dinner. Laughter flowed naturally, and sweet memories were made. It felt foreign at first, but I quickly fell in love with this new way of life.

For the next seventeen years—which were characterized by major moves in and out of the country and a rapidly growing family—we raised our children in an alcohol-free home. And somehow, I thought that my actions could write the story for my children—that through my sober living I could save them from the insidiousness of addiction. In 2008, something happened that made me realize my parental superhero cape was as make-believe as Cinderella's glass slipper.

It was an overcast February day. I set my empty coffee mug in the sink and grabbed my to-do notebook. *Grocery store,* I wrote but the jangle of the phone interrupted my next thought. I covered one ear with my free hand, straining to make out the hoarse whisper of my twenty-year-old son, Josh.

"Mom, I'm in detox. Can you and dad come get me?"

His quiet words ushered in another sound, the sound of my heart breaking.

Immediately my plans for the day changed as I abandoned the preparations for celebrating our oldest daughter's milestone birthday. Instead of grocery shopping for potatoes and steak and creating our family's special fancy cake—layers of spongy vanilla cake, raspberry yogurt cream, fresh raspberries, and shredded chocolate—I grabbed my jacket and followed Scott to the car.

The drive to the detox center at the hospital in Denver was only seven miles, but it seemed to take an eternity. I wrestled with a variety of emotions. Scott and I knew our son had recently started drinking—something he had never done in his teens. He no longer lived at home, so we weren't aware that his partying had quickly escalated. Even his drinking buddies had become concerned and would later share heart-breaking stories of Josh's drinking sprees. "What are you thinking?" Scott asked me as he drove. I'm rarely quiet when we are in the car, but that night my thoughts were a familiar lasso, choking me into silence. *How could I not know? What kind of mother am I?* "It's not your fault, you know," he said.

My husband knows me well. While a fierce and protective love for our children comes naturally to me, when it came to my daily parenting abilities, I often felt like I was fumbling in the dark. Scott's words pulled me from my introspection, and I turned to him. "Do you think this might be a turning point?" I asked. "That Josh might realize why we've warned him that addiction runs rampant in both of our families?" I grabbed at hope by thinking back to all the times God had used devastation to create something good in our lives.

"The main thing right now is that we get him home with us." Scott swerved to the right after nearly missing the turn for the hospital. "Later we can all talk, make a plan."

I nodded.

Josh was waiting in front of the hospital, and I tried to hide my shock at seeing him. Huddled against the cold, he looked wan and thin. I thought of the boy who used to sprint up the basement stairs and make me laugh with some antic or random joke, the young man who loved to cook and whose adventurous spirit once turned a winter blizzard into an opportunity to snowboard off the roof. I remembered the time he came home from a dinner out with friends so animated that his face practically lit up, all because he had been able to share Christ's love with a stranger in the restaurant. I had nicknamed him Joshie back when he was a toddler and even as an adult he enjoyed the name. The once animated boy had been replaced by a lethargic clone who could barely walk on his own. This was not my Joshie.

"Thanks," he croaked as Scott helped him into the car. The silence on the drive home was abruptly broken by gurgling sounds from the back seat. For a second time, Scott quickly yanked the steering wheel. He pulled off the road. My heart broke more as Josh spewed out of the rapidly rolled down window before leaning back against the seat and wiping his mouth. We stopped twice more on the way home. As the odor clinging to my second born child made its way to the front of the car, I gagged and rolled down my window despite the frigid temperature outside.

As soon as we got home, Scott helped Josh out of his jacket and into bed. He placed a trash can next to him and a cold washcloth over his eyes. I felt like a failure in a thousand and one ways. I believed I had failed Josh, and now I was failing my daughter on her special day.

Scott made a quick run to the grocery store for frozen french fries and steak while I hastily baked a cake, stopping now and again to brush away the tears that refused to stop.

Alyssa didn't complain but I knew that she was disappointed that her celebration had been disrupted—not to mention getting fries with her steak instead of the mashed potatoes she had requested. I tried to make it a fun evening in honor of the birthday girl, but it was difficult when we could hear her brother retching and moaning from the other room. We put candles on the not-so-fancy cake and sang happy birthday without much conviction.

Josh had already dropped out of college, but after that event we hoped he would return. Instead, he continued partying with new friends, and

Scott and I later learned he had moved beyond drinking to doing drugs. We couldn't seem to reach him.

During this time I fought my own personal battles. I fought against my own inability to save my kid from self-destruction. Against the self-blame that constantly sucker-punched me. And against a shocking anger with God. "What have I done wrong? Why won't You do something to rescue him?" I yelled in frustration at the Lord on more than one occasion. I kicked things. I tore up pages in my prayer and gratitude journal. I ranted and I raged, throwing things like a two-year-old who had missed her nap.

One Wednesday evening, I stayed home from church. I was in a wretched mood and having one of my "Why?" rages. I picked up a book titled *Promises of God* and threw it across my bedroom. The book landed spread eagle on top of my dresser and knocked over a cold cup of coffee. The smell of stale coffee seemed to match my bitter spirit as I watched it drip onto the carpet, doing nothing to stop it. Instead, I vented all my frustrations to the Lord. "We are raising our kids according to Your Word, Lord. Why am I again being crushed by someone else's decisions? Am I just not good enough? Where are Your promises? Your Word says You are a God of love, of impartiality, but I'm not feeling it. It seems like You prefer to bless others, and I keep getting hit."

Yes, I grumbled and complained. Yes, I yelled at the Lord. And when I finished my temper tantrum, I was too exhausted for anything except to listen to the Spirit's response: *Marie, you're concerned about what others will think of your parenting abilities. Most of this anger is about you and your image, not your children. It's pride.*

The words were like an ice-cold shower, shocking and not what I wanted or expected to hear. But it was true. I *did* think that my children reflected me. And I wanted to make sure that they mirrored a blemish-free image, that they made me look competent.

The Lord didn't stop there. Before I could even process the first truth, He went on: *You also think your kids are marionettes and that you hold the strings.*

"But, Lord," I defended myself, "aren't I responsible for how they turn out?"

My child, I am the perfect Parent and still my children rebel. YOU rebel. You are not responsible for another person's actions, only for following Me and walking in obedience.

In the coming weeks and months that simple but profound truth transformed my thinking more powerfully than anything since I had chosen to put my faith in the gospel of Jesus. I found myself returning to it time and time again. I had to remind myself: *I am in control of no one except myself. My role is to be still and listen to the Spirit and walk in constant fellowship with the Lord. To love unconditionally while living out my beliefs.* In other words, I could not prevent Josh—and later our youngest daughter—from drug addiction, but I could choose how I responded to it. I could be there to walk through the fire with them because God carries me. I could not prevent my oldest daughter's divorce or the anguish and tears that my young grandchildren—and their parents—experienced in the midst of it. But I could be a safe place for them to come with their pain and sorrow because I leaned into the Lord to comfort me in my own sorrow.

I am in control of no one except myself.

I have had to cling to that truth time and time again.

It has been a slow but constant letting go of the belief that I can argue, debate, wheedle, manipulate, or exhort anyone into doing what I think is best.

The hardest part about letting go has been watching my grown children falter in their faith—or even walk completely away from God. In fact, at this writing, none of my children are in church. Some have left the faith while others are deeply questioning. Initially I carried this burden on my own shoulders, and it nearly crippled me. I blamed myself for their crises of faith. Was it my parenting? The years of homeschooling? The transition to public schools? Had I been too strict? Too lenient? Were there not enough vacations? Had I said *yes* when I should have said *no,* and *no* when I should have said *yes?*

I thought of all the should-haves and could-haves. But what really kept me awake at night went beyond questioning my actions as a mother. It hit my identity and hit it hard. I found myself wondering if the decisions my kids were making about faith were rooted in how they viewed me as a person. *What if they are choosing a different way of life because they just don't like who I am as a person? What if they don't want anything to do with Scott and me as they move deeper into adulthood and different worldviews? Christ is at the very core of who I am, and now my kids are turning from Him. Does that mean they will turn away from me as well?* Once again, I felt as though I had failed. I was in a dark place and questioning everything about myself.

The truth is, I have a good relationship with each of my adult children. They all assure me that they had a wonderful, mostly carefree childhood. They come to me with sorrows, trials, and triumphs. I am so blessed to have them in my life, to have a relationship with them, and to hear them express gratitude for their growing up years. We have loud, noisy game nights and family dinners and birthday gatherings where more often than not we still make fancy cake, and the kids talk about their childhood. Still, my children don't accept what I know to be true: That the reason they had carefree childhoods was because Scott and I leaned on Scripture and actively sought guidance from God every day. Apart from His grace, we had no clue what healthy parenting looked like, and, left on our own, their childhoods would have been filled with chaos and brokenness, just like ours were.

I know I made mistakes as a mom. Lots of them. And I know I'm blessed that they have forgiven the mistakes. I give thanks regularly for the connection and closeness I have with my adult children. They are funny, smart, talented people. They inspire me and they teach me and challenge me to grow. I respect and admire them. I love them more fiercely than ever. But I had envisioned these later years in my life differently than what they are. I had pictured my huge family attending church together before coming home to boisterous Christmas Eve traditions of Rubens and wassail. I had pictured Easter sunrise services together before gathering around the table and gorging on sliced ham, mashed potatoes, and pumpkin pie topped with whipped cream. I pictured us praying together—kids and grandkids—and sharing how the Lord has been working in each of our lives. That isn't the way it is.

I don't let myself get weighed down by this. It has taken practice, but I can pray and release the responsibility for their beliefs because that responsibility isn't mine to carry. When I lean towards fretting or worry, I recall the truth God spoke to me back in 2008 when He said, *I am the perfect Parent and still my children rebel.* Shortly after that revelation, I carefully printed the names of my children on heart-shaped pieces of paper, wrote Jesus' name on another and tucked all the papers in a translucent envelope. I licked the envelope, sealing it closed, and glued a prayer of surrender on the outside. I put it on my desk where I could see it daily, a tangible reminder that ultimately my children are not mine.

Now that they are adults, I accept that their lives are not mine to direct. They make their own faith choices.

Recently a passage in Acts reminded me that even when people see the miraculous, they can choose to not accept it. In Acts 3, Peter and John healed a crippled man in the name of Jesus. Multitudes saw it and were astonished. So astonished that immediately afterwards, when Peter and John taught the people the good news of the gospel, thousands of the hearers became Christ followers.

But not everyone who saw the miracle believed it. The big-wigs in Jerusalem—the rulers, elders, and teachers of the law—were furious and arrested Peter and John. They demanded to know by what power or authority the two men had done these things. The account says that Peter, being filled with the Holy Spirit, gave a bold witness of Jesus Christ of Nazareth.

The man who had been healed was standing with Peter and John. These leaders saw the man with their own eyes. Scripture says they couldn't deny his healing. *They saw the miracle.* A man who had been unable to walk since birth—for forty years! —was suddenly jumping and leaping and praising God. A miracle. But these leaders chose not to accept it and instead, after a private conference, came back and told Peter and John they weren't allowed to speak or teach in the name of Christ.

Today people can still see a miracle standing right in front of them and choose to deny it, to believe another explanation. That's what free will is all about. We are all given a choice. My children are not exempt from this, and they get to choose for themselves what they believe. They have seen and acknowledged a total transformation in my life, but they see it as something other than a miracle of Christ.

I can't change that. I can only live out Christ in me.

This continues to be a tough but liberating truth for me to accept. I don't get to control or make choices for anyone else, including my children.

And I certainly couldn't control the gunman who burst into a movie theater and sprayed seventy-six bullets, savagely massacring twelve people, and physically injuring seventy others.

12: The Aurora Theater Massacre

JULY 19 BEGAN AS A DECEPTIVELY SUNNY DAY. It arrived like a pigtailed girl, fidgeting impatiently on the front porch, asking, "Can you come out and play?" I wanted to say yes. I wanted to unearth chlorine faded swimsuits and raggedy beach towels, and drive Michelle, Elizabeth, and myself to Alyssa's apartment a few miles away. The thought of lounging around the seldom crowded apartment pool with my daughters was almost irresistible. But I had things to do.

At nine o'clock I needed to drive Michelle to her summer job, and I really needed to do something about the empty refrigerator. I also wanted to do some job hunting. Instead of making plans for enjoying the cloudless summer day, I busied myself with creating a to-do list: Search cookbooks for pescetarian (fish only) recipes. Make a grocery list. Go to Sam's Club and Sprouts. Schedule a dentist appointment. Do another job search through the APS website. Just ordinary, everyday tasks.

I sighed and got to work.

Had I known just how far from ordinary our next few days and weeks were going to be, I would have grabbed those swimsuits. Had I realized we were about to experience a dark night that would forever change us, I would have ignored the to-dos altogether and headed out into the sunshine. The details of life, however, are not written out for us by an illustrious playwright. I had no well-scripted foreshadowing of the evil that would demolish our mundane routine, or of the darkness that would fall upon us.

That morning there was only sunshine. Glorious, abundant sunshine. So when Michelle hollered downstairs to me that she was ready to go, I grabbed my purse and headed out the door to drop her off at work.

"I can't wait to go see the midnight showing of *The Dark Knight Rises* tonight," my middle daughter said as she slid out of the Focus. "Though I bet *you* aren't quite as excited." She grinned impishly and waved good-bye. I watched her slim figure saunter away, youthful exuberance and innocence worn as casually as the towel about her neck. I watched until she disappeared into the old brick school building where she would spend the next three hours trying to teach a bunch of rambunctious seven-year-olds how to swim. I let the car idle for a few more moments and wondered exactly when she had transformed into this long-legged, confident young woman. In my mind, I still saw her as the freckle-faced adolescent who loved *Little House on the Prairie,* backyard forts, paper-dolls, and climbing trees I sighed again.

Nostalgia is such a funny companion; it arrives as an aching sadness dressed in delightful memories. Watching each of my children reach the cusp of adulthood had always been bittersweet. I loved the deepening, transitioning relationships. I loved the noise and energy of a home filled with teenagers and young adults. But sometimes I longed for the chubby arms and legs and incessant chattering, the mornings at the playground, and the afternoons teaching pliable minds to sound out words and memorize multiplication tables. It has been a lingering and wistful farewell to bedtime stories and Play Doh and tents created with blankets in the living room.

Having children was never on my original to-do list. God, with His wonderfully kind sense of humor, saw fit to make me a walking advertisement for abstinence being the only sure method of birth control. He gave me not one, not two, but *six* kids in a matter of eleven years.

My children have brought me a deeper fulfillment and greater joy than I could have envisioned. But parenting did not come naturally to me, and I have fumbled my way through much of it. Certainly, we have had tumultuous times—seasons when I wondered if the heartbreak would ever end, parenting winters when I could do nothing but cry out for God's grace and drought-like summers when I wondered if I would ever get this mothering thing right.

Fortunately, winters are always followed by spring, rain eventually soaks the parched summer ground, and children are always, always worth the emotional costs. I had to learn that my Savior is capable of filling in the holes left by my parenting mistakes. I now know the best way I can parent is by letting Christ transform me and then let Him love my children through me. I just wish it hadn't taken me so long to learn that lesson. By that time, three of my children had already flown the coop, and I was bracing for eighteen-year-old Matthew to follow suit at the end of the summer. Soon only Michelle, sixteen, and Elizabeth, fourteen, would still be at home.

The years seemed to have evaporated, leaving this lingering layer of remember whens, and I didn't want to waste the precious few seconds I had left with them under my wing. Which is why I had offered to take Michelle and Elizabeth to the premier of *Batman: The Dark Knight Rises,* a movie they had been talking about for months.

I didn't particularly like going to movie theaters. I preferred relaxing in a recliner and reading a book. Or at least watching movies in the comfort of my own home where I could sprawl out on the sofa and get a foot rub from my husband. I especially disliked action movies. And I really, really disliked midnight showings. But parenting means making sacrifices; it means sometimes laying aside my own desires for the desires of the people I love. And this was such a small sacrifice. Even if I didn't enjoy the movie, I would get to spend time with my daughters doing something that would make them happy.

Around five that evening, Scott and I sat around our large, distressed dinner table with Matthew, Michelle, and Elizabeth devouring perfectly grilled salmon, fresh strawberries, a tossed salad, and rolls dripping with butter. The conversation turned to the night's anticipated adventure. "It's nearly sold out," Matthew warned us. "You may want to get your tickets now." He and his friends would be attending the same *Batman* premiere and had already purchased their tickets online.

"Can you go online and buy tickets for us?" I asked.

Matthew, who is much quicker at any maneuvers on the computer than I am, readily agreed. I handed him my debit card. An email instructed us to pick up our three tickets at the Century 16 Theater in Aurora Colorado for the 12:05 a.m. showing of *The Dark Knight Rises*.

We were assigned to theater nine. Matthew and his friends had been assigned to theater eight.

At 5:59 p.m. we printed out the receipt for the tickets and then began clearing the dinner table. As soon as the dishwasher was humming, I decided to sit down and write a quick blog post about the new pescatarian eating adventure on which Elizabeth and I had embarked. I titled the post *"You're a WHAT? Parenting is All About Making Sacrifices . . . but Bacon?!"* It started as a lighthearted look at giving up meat to support my daughter's new culinary lifestyle but ended with a serious reminder about the ultimate sacrifice Jesus had made for humankind, the laying down of His life.

At 7:08 I hit the publish button. I had no idea that six hours later, I would be relying on that sacrificial gift of Christ to give me peace in the midst of horror. And that I would be faced with the possibility of sacrificing my own life to save the lives of my daughters.

At 7:20 Elizabeth and Michelle tried to convince me that it wasn't too early to head to the theater. I was not persuaded. "We already have tickets reserved so an hour will give us plenty of time," I told them. "We'll leave just before 11 o'clock." I didn't want to spend more than an hour sitting in uncomfortable theater seats.

"Okay," the girls sighed.

"Want to go for a walk to make the time go by quicker?" Elizabeth asked her older sister who nodded in agreement.

"You'll have to go now and be home before it gets dark," I told them. "Or take the dog with you."

"Mom, Zeke's a pain for us to walk," Michelle said. "He only does well with Matthew. We'll go now, and we promise to be back before dark."

Sometimes my children have complained that I am too protective, too strict. It has been one of my biggest parenting struggles—finding that paper thin balance between allowing them freedom to grow while providing safe boundaries and protection—and I have often fallen on the side of overprotection. I can see it *now*. Just like in the past when I thought I was responsible for their health and their life choices, I thought if I controlled their circumstances and environments, I could keep them safe. That illusion of control and protection would be shattered within hours.

At 8:15 Matthew and I were reading in the living room. I closed my book. "I'm really not looking forward to a midnight movie." I didn't realize I had spoken out loud until Matthew responded.

"Hey, I only have one person riding with me, everyone else is meeting us there. I have plenty of room in my car if Michelle and Elizabeth want to go with me. We won't be in the same theater, but the girls could ride there and back with me if you really don't want to go," he suggested.

It was a tempting offer, but it didn't feel right. *Just go with your girls like you planned,* something inside of me said. "Thanks for the offer, but I'll go with them."

"Okay," Matthew shrugged.

I spent the next two hours puttering around, doing a bit of laundry, reading, and playing scrabble on my Kindle.

At 10:50 I told the girls we could leave.

"Do you have the receipt? And your credit card?" Michelle asked.

"Got 'em," I said, waving the Fandango receipt. I grabbed my purse and Kindle, and we headed out. "I should have just let you ride with Matthew," I said with a grin as I pulled my seat forward. Michelle turned the radio to an eardrum-splitting level, and we sang along with artists on K-Love.

Less than ten minutes later, I pulled into the north parking lot of the theater. I assumed this parking lot would be practically empty since it was on the side of the theater and was surprised to find it more than half full. The girls bounced out of the car, and I followed them into the doors below a brightly lit, abstract sign announcing Century 16.

"Wow! I guess we should have come sooner," I told the girls as we stared in dismay at the long, winding queue. When we finally reached the teller, I handed over my credit card which was quickly returned with three printed tickets. The time was 11:22 p.m.

The smell of buttery popcorn was tempting, but the girls and I avoided the concessions, swerved to the right, and headed to Theater 9. We rounded the corner into the dimly lit room and glanced up at the old, stadium-style seats. We stopped abruptly. Once again, we were confronted with people. Lots of people. The place was packed.

Other than the first few rows practically beneath the screen, we spied only one other area where we could sit together. I quickly headed towards the five empty seats less than halfway up. I let Michelle enter the row first, and I was about to pull my own seat bottom down when a young man from the other end of the row called out to us.

"Hey, we were really trying to save this row for our friends." He was pleasant but firm.

I looked around and groaned. "But there aren't any other spots with three seats together, except in the very front." I let my tone of voice plead the full argument for me. There was no way I wanted to have to stare straight up at the screen for two hours.

"Aw, c'mon, man. We don't even know if the others are coming," another young man called out. "Let 'em sit there." I lifted up a silent thank you to the Lord, as well as an audible one towards our unidentified advocate, and plopped myself down between my two daughters.

The movie crowd was noisy, and I hoped some of the energy of the room would fall on me. Several people were wearing attention-grabbing batman costumes. I was surprised at the great lengths to which the mostly young crowd had gone to dress up for the premiere. A young couple approached our aisle. Elizabeth was on the very end of the row, with me in the middle, and Michelle on my other side. There were two empty seats between Michelle and the young man who had wanted to save the entire row for his friends. "Is anyone sitting there?" The dark-haired woman pointed. I glanced down to check with Mr. Seat Saver before I gave the go-ahead. I planned to scoot down so they could have the aisle seats. But before I could respond, the couple slid past me and settled in the seats next to Michelle.

Finally, the little video clip reminding movie goers to turn off their cell phones silenced the crowd for a few seconds. I was not prepared for the enthusiasm of midnight moviegoers. Throughout the previews for a new TV series and a few upcoming movies, excitement permeated the air. It was contagious, and I surprised myself by joining in and cheering during *The Hobbit* clips. The festive mood reached a boisterous climax when the preview for *Superman: Man of Steel* filled the screen and a few people competitively shouted out the name of Spiderman.

The moment the feature film *Batman: The Dark Knight Rises* began, my eyes were glued to the screen. Still, I couldn't figure out what was going on. The noise and nonstop movement on-screen felt chaotic to me. I squirmed in my seat. Suddenly I heard a sizzling noise followed by a loud pop. An object went flying across the room, smoke trailing from it. People shouted in anger at the interruption. My girls started to cough. Flabbergasted by what I assumed was some kind of special effects prank, I turned my attention back to the movie. I stared at the screen, still trying to figure out the plot.

Suddenly the theater was filled with shrieks and cries. Next to me, Michelle and Elizabeth began screaming. "Mom! What's happening? What's going on?" Scanning the room in panic, I saw a dark figure standing about fifty feet in front of us. A man. Or woman. With a gun.

Shots started coming, rapid and nonstop. I opened my mouth, but no sound came out. All around me were the frantic voices of terrified people. "Get down! Get down!" Michelle and I finally screamed at the same time. The two of us dropped to our stomachs on the sticky floor in front of our seats. I yanked Elizabeth down with me.

Omigosh, omigosh, Elizabeth is at the end of the aisle! My heart froze. *If the shooter walks up the aisle, she is the closest to him.*

The possibility of a bullet striking my fourteen-year-old daughter sent a jolt through me as though I had been struck. I lifted myself up and threw my body over hers, praying that my tiny frame would be enough of a cushion to save her life should a bullet hit us.

Sweating and terrified, my body was taut, expecting a bullet at any moment. With my face pressed into the dirty carpet, I had no idea where the shooter was. Adrenaline kept me from noticing any impact from the chemical bomb that the gunman had initially thrown, but both of my daughters were choking and gasping, unable to catch their breath.

The screams of the wounded, terrorized people trying to make sense of the senseless, and the quieter but equally traumatic whimpering would reverberate in my mind for days. Their echoes would be heard for eternity.

The high pitch screeching of the building's emergency sirens added to the horror of the moment.

Shortly after we hit the floor, there was a momentary silence from the gun or guns, and I began to hope the nightmare was over. Instead, the shots, like booming firecrackers, resumed. They went on and on and on. I was freaking out, certain that this was it. This was how my life was going to end, on a dirty theater floor while crushing my daughter.

Whimpering and shaking, I began to whisper out loud, at first just speaking the name of Jesus over and over. Suddenly a peace that transcends human understanding swept over me. I `realized that I was ready to die. Not that I wanted to die. And not that I relished the idea of physical pain—I hoped if a fatal bullet struck, death would come quickly. But I was confident that if I breathed my last breath on earth, I would be in the present of Jesus and my heart actually quickened at the thought. *Death was not to be feared!*

This realization strengthened me, and I continued praying out loud. I prayed for peace and protection for those in the theater. I prayed for the shooting and carnage to stop. Mostly I repeated the name of my Redeemer over and over. At the same time, in the back of my mind I wondered what a bullet ripping through my flesh would feel like and how my children would get through the grief of being motherless.

As I prayed, the rapid-fire shots again abruptly stopped. I sensed Michelle getting up, and I turned my head in her direction. Others were clamoring to their feet all around us. *"Run!"* Michelle screamed and took off. I pushed myself off Elizabeth and yanked her to her feet. People were trying to make their way to the exit doors behind us, screeching at us to run, shoving and pushing us in their own panicked attempts to flee.

I had no idea where the shooter was, or if there was more than one. I lost sight of Michelle and scrambled in her direction, pulling an almost catatonic Elizabeth behind me. "Michelle! Michelle!" my throat burned as I shouted for my sixteen-year-old. As I searched for her, bloodied people half ran, half stumbled past me. I continued babbling prayers and calling her name. I spotted her as soon as we got through the exit door at the top of a staircase and grabbed her hand.

The light outside the theater room was blinding. We stumbled down the stairs. "Run, run, run!" I screamed. "And watch for shooters." Adrenaline was flowing and all I could think of was getting my daughters to safety.

As we sped through the lobby, it was hard to comprehend what was going on. People were screaming and running, some limping with blood streaming down them, clutching an arm or holding a hand over their face. *This can't be happening; this can't be happening.* My mind now split into a dozen directions. *Are Matthew and his friends safe? I'm running with only one of my new Crocs on. Please, please don't let my girls be struck. Is this the act of some vengeful, slighted lover against his or her ex? Can we make it to the car? Is there more than one gunman? Are there shooters outside?*

We followed the stream of people out the main door of the theater. I didn't feel the pavement on my bare foot as we sprinted towards the parking lot and our car. I spied our little red Focus, and my consuming thought was to get the girls inside so they would have some protection if bullets started flying. Several police cars sat in front of the theater. Their lights were flashing in an eerie rhythm with the emergency alarms, and we could hear the wail of more sirens in the distance.

It felt like we were characters in a horror movie. That's when shock set in.

Out of breath, I dumped my purse onto the trunk of my car and frantically searched for the keys. Seconds later, I heard the clicking sound that signaled unlocked doors and I blubbered "Thank you," as tears and mucous streamed down my face. I tossed the purse and its contents into the car and screamed at the girls to get in. "Call Matthew. Call Matthew and make sure they are okay!" I alternately whimpered and shouted. Michelle fumbled with her phone and moments later reached her brother.

"They're okay, they're okay," Michelle's voice was amped and hysterical. "They are on their way home."

Meanwhile, Elizabeth made several attempts with shaking fingers to phone her dad. His shift began at four in the morning. I knew he would be sound asleep, but she finally got through. I could tell from her end of the conversation that he didn't understand her cries. He had no clue what was going on. "But we're okay, we're okay," Elizabeth kept repeating, and I knew she was trying to persuade herself.

I started the car, turned on the lights, and sped out of the parking lot. A minute later, we passed a chain of fifteen or twenty police cars, making its way like a flashing snake towards the Aurora Century 16 Theater.

I drove with one hand covering my mouth, trying to hold in the whimpers that kept escaping. The girls were mostly silent, their minds trying to process all that they had seen and heard. When we got home, the girls and I were still in shock. We tried to explain to Scott what happened, but it sounded like gibberish.

"Something went flying through the air, some chemical. Then there were gunshots, tons of gunshots, and we all hit the floor." I forced the words out while my brain struggled to make sense of what I was saying. Did it really happen? It couldn't possibly have happened. That is the stuff of horror movies, not real life. Not *my* life.

We checked social media to see if anyone was sharing anything and our feeds were blowing up. The devastation was real. The shock began to wear off and panic hit. "Oh my gosh!" I cried, reading the fast-paced updates. "The shooter rigged his apartment building with chemicals and explosives hoping to blow it up and keep the police busy. What if he put bombs under the cars in the parking lot?"

I had all kinds of crazy thoughts and hysteria was rising like an out-of-control roller coaster. "Kyle, will you check under the car? Quickly?" Our oldest son had recently returned from a war zone, and I was sure he would know what explosives looked like. He acquiesced, heading out to the driveway without even bothering to put on his shoes. My heart slowed down a bit when he came back in with an all clear.

The hours and days following the carnage at the theater passed in a surreal haze. I was both exhausted and hyped up. In the midst of many expected emotions, something else rose up. I felt great indignation at all of the people using this horrific event to blame God. In my frustration, I penned a quick blogpost:

> God didn't do this. He gives mankind freewill and sometimes man chooses evil. Why would you think such a tragedy would make me question the goodness of God? He isn't the cause of evil, but the One who can bring comfort and peace in the midst of the most horrific events.

It was then, in those moments of pouring out my heart that I let go of the final thread of control—the *illusion* of control—that I still clutched. It was both terrifying and liberating to recognize that *anything* could happen at *any time.*

A tragedy beyond anything my mind had ever dreamt up had indeed ripped into my world. But God had carried me through. God continues to carry me through. My faith was intact. More than intact, it had been tested and strengthened.

I would still struggle with PTSD for years. I had a panic attack the first time I entered a JC Penney store several weeks after the shooting. I entered through one of the side doors of the store, right next to racks of colorful petite dresses and blouses with a 30 percent off sign beckoning me. I reached for a marine-blue, button up polyester blouse but suddenly the thought of being in a mall full of strangers stole my breath. I turned around and half walked, half ran out of the store.

For months afterwards, whenever I grocery shopped, I experienced panic attacks. One moment I would be checking out the ripeness of pineapples or avocados and the next minute my hands would turn clammy, and I was scanning the aisles for a safe place to drop to the floor and hide if necessary.

I had nightmares.

Loud noises—particularly cars backfiring, balloons popping, fireworks exploding—would cause my body to tense. I experienced deep, deep grief for the twelve people who lost their lives. Stitched to the grief was a sense of guilt. Every time I read about six-year-old Veronica losing her life in such a horrific manner, I wept until my eyeballs hurt and there were no tears left inside of me.

"Why? Why her and not me?" I cried out to the Lord. "Why any of them?" I felt guilty for not running back into the theater and trying to rescue others. While my faith in God was still intact, mental battles and questions raged on. I didn't get all the answers I desperately sought. But each time that I brought my fears, questions, and sorrows to the Lord, peace stepped in and swathed me, much like the moment I lay on that dirty theater carpet and could do nothing except cry out the name of

Jesus. It was a peace so powerful and visceral it felt as though the Lord were singing a lullaby over me.

I would hold fast to that soothing lullaby and supernatural peace in the months to follow when yet another cataclysmic event—the death of my mother—shifted the ground beneath my feet.

13: Losing Mom

THE CALL FROM MY SISTER CAME ON FRIDAY, SEPTEMBER 28, exactly ten weeks after the theater shooting. "I think you need to head to Vermont." Her voice cracked and I could tell she had been crying. "It's time. Hospice says mom's organs are shutting down. It could be days or hours."

The next morning I boarded an airplane with my youngest daughter. Thirty minutes into the flight, we hit a storm, and it felt like we were on a roller coaster rather than an airplane. Elizabeth looked like she was going to pass out. She gripped my hand tightly, but I barely felt it. My thoughts were as turbulent as the flight, and I was caught in my own storm of emotions.

Please, Lord, give her more time. I need more time. You know I planned to spend time with her at the end of the month. Please don't let this be it, I silently cried as I thought back to something that had happened shortly after the theater shooting.

Just when I had felt like I was back on firmer emotional footing, I experienced the strangest little breakdown. Scott arrived home from work to find me huddled in our bed, sobbing uncontrollably. "I just want my mom," I told him, feeling confused and disconcerted, like I had been transported back to adolescence, back to the apartment on Province Street and the nights when Crazy George raged in the apartment below ours. Nights when I just wanted the safety of my mom's presence.

Needing my mom was an odd, barely remembered sensation for me. I had left my home state of Vermont in the 1980s when I joined the Air Force, and I had never looked back. Through the decades since, my mom and I wrote letters and spoke on the phone. She sent furniture and gifts when I was preparing to be a single mom stationed in Florida. She mailed me a brand-new sewing machine when I got married. I dreamed of becoming as skilled with it as she was, but without her guidance I never really made an effort.

I had returned to Richford for brief visits, particularly in the earlier years. But having six children in an eleven-year span ushered in a whirlwind of sleep deprivation, constant activity, and extremely tight finances. As the years passed, and I kept spitting out children, it became too difficult and too expensive for me to fly everyone across the country.

Mom visited me one time, in 1989 or 1990, when Scott and I were living in Florida and had just the two boys. She and her husband were embarking on a ten-day cruise and had arranged to leave my not-so-baby sister Jessie with us to enjoy some southern sunshine while they vacationed.

That brief time my mom spent with my family in Florida was the first and last time she would visit us. She didn't come before or after any of my children were born, but I brushed away the tinges of sadness that pinched my heart each time she missed out on such momentous occasions. I got used to it, got caught up in the life of homeschooling six children and constant sleepovers, sports activities, and an always bursting-at-the-seams home life. A full and vibrant life that didn't leave time to dwell on the fact that apart from cards on holidays and special occasions, and the twice-a-month phone calls, my mom didn't have much involvement in my life. But still there was a little hollow spot in my heart and I used to wipe away tears whenever I read the children's book *Are You My Mother?* to my young children. I felt pangs of envy whenever my friends would enjoy visits from *their* moms who loved doting on their grandchildren. When the mom of one of my best friends got to know my kids and asked about them by name whenever she called her daughter, it felt bittersweet to me. I appreciated it, but it shined a spotlight on that empty spot in my life and in my kids' life.

Maybe I should have done more, pushed more. I'd made some feeble efforts. I once sent my mom one of those *Tell Me About You, Mom* books, but she never filled it out. I didn't really expect her to, but I had hoped to have stories to share with my children.

In 2009, Scott and I had taken our youngest four children who were still living at home on a Vermont vacation. It had been my kids' first taste of small-town, country living. They'd spent their days hanging out with cousins they had never met. They rode horses, got up close and friendly with some cows in a family member's barn, and went four wheeling for the first time. It had also been my kids' first time getting to know their Grandma Lil in person—two had been babies when she had last seen them, and two she had never met. Unfortunately, the "getting to know" time was limited because my mother's health was already failing. Sadly, it was not only the first time my younger children got to know my mother, but also—as I had suspected—the last. I felt no regret that we spent thousands of dollars on the trip.

So yeah, I lived most of my adult life without leaning on my mother— or my father—for any help or advice and then, suddenly, during the weeks after the shooting I wanted my mom the way a newborn cries out for the nurturing touch of its mom. But she didn't even call me.

I received cards and letters and emails and packages from strangers all around the world, but from my mom there was silence. I was crushed. Until the day I'd tossed my twentieth soggy tissue in the trash, and I realized the truth. She *couldn't* call. It wasn't that she didn't care or that she didn't want to comfort me. She was dying from COPD and other health issues. She struggled for breath. In the aftermath of the shooting, even if she had wanted to be there for me, she simply couldn't. She was physically incapable.

That led to another cathartic epiphany. During my childhood, even if my mom longed to be there for me emotionally, she simply couldn't.

She was incapable because she was struggling to survive her own battles. My mom's mother and a brother died in a car accident when she was just seven years old. Seven! She was an innocent little girl whose world was turned upside down. She went to live with a sister until my grandfather remarried.

I cannot fathom how traumatic that childhood loss must have been, a loss that wouldn't—couldn't—ever really go away. That little seven-year-old girl must have cried for days, weeks, months. Years. I had long ago let go of any anger or wounds from my own growing up years, but now I went deeper, beyond forgiveness and compassion into empathy. My heart broke anew because of my mother's childhood loss, for what it stole from her as a little girl, and what it stole from her as a beautiful, grown woman.

My mom had also suffered another major loss. She lost another brother to a tragic drowning just before she graduated high school. I can't imagine what that must have been like, the herculean strength it must have taken to get through a valedictorian speech when she had just laid her brother to rest.

She lost two of her fingers in a snowmobile accident.

And my mom became a mother herself at a young age, giving birth to a son and two daughters within a span of just under twenty-three months. She would later give birth to three more children.

When my father's constant infidelity and other issues, became too much to bear, she found herself a divorced mother who bore most of the responsibility of raising six children by herself. She must have been terrified. Exhausted. She must have felt helpless and hopeless much of the time. I imagine her lying awake at night, wondering *how am I going to get through this?* And back in her day, there weren't resources readily available like we have today. People buried their emotions, ignored them and sometimes drank them away. Looking back, I am amazed that she could function at all, amazed that she still had such a kind and tender heart towards so many people.

After the theater shooting, during that season of emotional breakdown, I understood why she didn't—or couldn't—call me. But I longed to see her, to hug her, and, in the midst of my own healing, to tell her again in person how deeply sorry I was for all that she went through as a young person and how brave and strong and beautiful she was.

Less than a month after the shooting rampage, I started working for Aurora public schools, so I scheduled a visit to Vermont to see my mom during my fall break. I looked forward to the October visit, for the opportunity to delve into some deep conversations that she had acknowledged were difficult for her. But now, sitting on the most turbulent flight I'd ever been on, gripping Elizabeth's hand and asking God to give me more time with my mom, I realized those conversations may never happen. I realized my mom likely wasn't going to make it until then. It felt like a race against time.

We landed at the itty-bitty airport in Burlington, Vermont. I barely remember getting picked up and driven to my sister's home, where Elizabeth and I dropped our suitcases and headed a few houses down to my mom's apartment.

Mom was no longer coherent. She passed away forty hours later, on a cold and rainy October day. I was grateful that I could be there, grateful that I was able to climb into her bed and lie next to her gaunt body. Grateful for the chance to whisper that I loved her. Still, a deep grief for all that we had both missed out on hung over me.

I had visited her the year before, in 2011. After my visit she had shared with me that she had entrusted her life and soul to Jesus. I am thankful she voiced that to me. Although I felt her earthly life had been cut too short, I knew I would see her again in heaven. Even with that knowledge, it would take years for me to release the grief to the Lord who began to transform it into the abiding peace that comes from finally letting go. The peace that comes from the ongoing process of releasing past wounds and future worries, the peace that carries power on its shoulders and joy in its hands.

I'm getting to live out the truth of God's word that says although I will have troubles and fiery trials in this world, I can still live boldly because *no matter what* I have an empowering peace from Him who never leaves me. And much more than that, I have joy.

The Christian life seems to make no sense logically. It is an upside-down way of living. It is a life that is antithetical to much of the world's ways. Yet in living upside down, I have discovered abundance like I never imagined. I experienced it during the season when my husband confessed his pornography addiction. When I thought my dream marriage was over, I discovered this marvelous truth that God can take what appears hopeless and dead and breathe new, stronger, better life into it. I experienced it when I became a bondservant to Christ, and He set me free to live in triumphant joy. When I was at my weakest, I discovered strength beyond my own capabilities. And when facing the darkest, coldest of seasons, God covered me with a comforting garment stitched with peace and joy, a garment stitched by the Light of the world Himself. I continue to experience it today.

It all began with letting go of the illusion of control and freefalling into the grace of God. When I learned how to do that, it brought me to the very life I had fought in vain to create on my own. The changes that have come from walking in the Spirit have been deep and visceral. And those internal changes have manifested themselves in noticeable, outward changes, especially to those closest to me.

PART FIVE:

INTO ABUNDANCE

The thief does not come except to steal and kill and destroy.
I have come that they may have life and have it more abundantly.
– Jesus (John 10:10 NKJV, circa AD 30-33)

14: Freefalling

IN 2017, I DECIDED IT WAS TIME FOR A TANGIBLE STEP TO CELEBRATE this beautiful paradox of letting go and discovering abundance, of breaking free from all the layers of self-protection and trying to control. At the same time, I also wanted to commemorate the fifth anniversary of the Aurora Century16 tragedy in a way that showed evil doesn't win. Fear doesn't win.

I didn't want to skulk around in the middle of July, handling the anniversary in the way I handled emotional struggles in years past. I didn't want to be awkwardly wielding childhood coping mechanisms that never worked anyway. I didn't want to leave the sadness and survivor's guilt buried down inside, twisting into that old familiar rope that silenced my vocal cords. I didn't want to avoid people simply because I still cry when I remember the horror of that night, and I detest crying in front of people. I didn't want to distract myself by rearranging furniture or creating other projects to escape the memories.

I didn't want to give in to any of that anymore.

I knew there was a better way to face the day, a way to meet it head-on with courage, connection, and communion. I texted my daughters Michelle and Elizabeth, who also struggled every July: "Hey, let's go skydiving on the anniversary this year."

143

After they overcame their shock at my suggestion, they agreed it was a great idea. I made reservations for the afternoon of July 20. When I told my astounded husband what I had done, he offered to tag along for moral support.

While waiting on the tarmac for the flatbed trailer that would take us to the plane, I paced and checked the time on my phone. I texted a photo of my daughters and myself in skydiving gear to one of my girlfriends and then to my three sisters through our Facebook group chat affectionately named Fab4. I paced some more and then glanced over at Michelle and Elizabeth to see how they were faring. One looked sick, the other somewhat excited.

The July Colorado heat was making me sweat in the heavy skydiving jumpsuit, melting the little bit of makeup I had applied that morning. I fought against the sick feeling deep in my stomach and slapped away the thought of bolting.

I can do all things through Christ who gives me strength, I repeated to myself while Scott gave my hand a squeeze.

Months ago, I'd told him, "What better way to demonstrate that fear doesn't have control than to step into the fear?" I had sounded so confident back then when the actual jump was still in the distant future. But now that the day was here, now that we had each handed over two hundred dollars for a six-minute thrill, I was as doubtful as Scott had been.

More than doubtful. Panic tapped on my shoulder. What had I been thinking?

I took a deep breath and reminded myself fear had no control on my life. Finally, Scott, Elizabeth, Michelle, and I climbed onto the trailer and endured a dusty, bumpy ride to the spot where we would board the plane.

A short time later, we met our tandem instructors. After some chit-chat and basic instructions, we boarded a twin engine jet-prop plane in the order in which we would jump. My instructor, and I were last.

The pilot decided to leave the aircraft door open, so we could watch the ascent. I wished he hadn't. I prayed for Elizabeth who looked ready to throw up. I was certain I looked the same way.

The plane was rapidly reaching an altitude of 18,000 feet above sea level. I watched everything below me turn into miniatures and the smaller the buildings got, the faster my heart beat. *What if I back out at the very last minute?* I wondered.

I joked with my instructor in a futile attempt to cover the fear. He asked a lot of questions. I could tell he was used to terrified jumpers and knew how to calm them. He assured me he had done thousands of successful jumps. While we talked, he snapped our harnesses together. Although still scared, I trusted him.

Michelle and her instructor moved from their seats to the open door. The instructor gave a signal and then the two of them were falling out of the plane. My heart fell with them until I saw the parachute open, and they slowed to a graceful glide.

My instructor and I slid towards the door. When Elizabeth and her instructor reached it, the look on my daughter's face still mirrored the terror I felt. She bravely nodded that she was ready, and I watched in disbelief as her instructor led them in a flip out of the aircraft. Again, I held my breath until I saw the parachute open.

My instructor and I scooted to the door. I looked down and my heart thudded so loudly I thought it would shake the plane. I tried to remember all the instructions about keeping my arms crossed at my chest and my legs bent. I nodded, my instructor rocked back and forth and then we were falling.

Free falling.

For approximately sixty-seconds we fell five thousand feet at 130 miles per hour.

It was the most terrifying yet exhilarating moment I had ever experienced.

And then my instructor pulled the cords of the parachute. With the colorful umbrella above us, we slowed to a gentle ten miles per hour, and I looked down.

My thoughts weren't on the past or the future but totally caught up in the adrenaline rush of the present. It was such an incredible and liberating feeling, literally falling into my greatest fear, and ultimately discovering joy, beauty, courage, and excitement. The next five minutes were a paradox. They sped by while seeming interminable. As we approached solid ground, the temperature rose. By the time we landed, the heat was stifling, nauseating even. After my instructor unhitched us from the parachute and each other, I bent over and dry heaved. I spent most of the drive home bent over in my seat with a plastic bag in my hands. No one had warned me about the motion sickness that often occurs with a jump.

But I would do it all again in a heartbeat because those sixty seconds of free falling symbolized for me my entire faith walk. I don't need to be in control. I never really was, anyway.

I can let go of what was merely an illusion and remain in tandem with the trustworthy One. Free falling with the Lord has allowed me to embrace the abundant life He has created for me, the life He has created *me for*. A life of inner peace, joy, and contentment *no matter the circumstances*. With the Lord, I can head into the unknown courageously and expectantly.

Because we always end up in a place of abundance.

Likewise, I can let go of any façade, and of any worry about being broken open, because I'm no longer hollow inside. I'm filled with the greatest treasure—the glorious, empowering Spirit of God.

December 2021

My phone vibrates, and I glance at the incoming text from my son Matthew. "I'm not sure if we are going to make it in time. Traffic is horrible."

I text back. "I'll leave your tickets at the check-in table. We are going to go ahead and get seats since it is already crowded."

It is my granddaughter's first ballet recital, and all our in-state immediate family members plan to be here, cheering her on. Scott and I reach the table where we are to trade our tickets for green *X*s on our hands.

"My son and granddaughter are running late," I tell a silver haired lady wearing a Santa hat. "Can we leave their tickets here?"

"I'm happy to keep their tickets for them," she smiles. "But as soon as the doors close, we won't be letting anyone in because it is a distraction for the dancers."

I lift a silent prayer for my son to arrive in time.

We file in and find seats as close to the front as we can. Our group— Scott and I, four of our children, a son-in-love, and two of our four grandchildren—fill most of the row. I look around at the crowd filling the large school auditorium and sigh with relief when Matthew and Ophie slip in beside Elizabeth.

As sometimes happens when I am in a crowded room of strangers, I panic. *This is the perfect environment for a mass shooting.* The thought lasts for a fraction of a second before I breathe deeply, smile, and take my husband's hand.

My granddaughter is in her happy place when she prances out on stage in a red-and-white candy-striped dress. Her normally unruly hair is pulled back into a thick ponytail and held with a large, red bow. I can't help crying. Happy tears, because I get to be there for this moment in their lives, and I know how close I came to not being here. I taste the saltiness of the tears and do not wipe them away.

The kids onstage are adorable. Though sometimes out of step or off key, their dancing and singing are earnest and heartfelt, and the audience roars in delight. Afterwards, we take photos in front of a cardboard candy house. My favorite picture is of my four grandchildren, arms around each other, grinning from ear to ear. My oldest grandson, at eight years old, has opted to wear a long tie over his plaid, button up shirt in honor of the event, and it hangs askew. His younger brother is sporting a bow tie and polo shirt. The youngest granddaughter, in a unicorn dress, is beaming up at her ballet-performing cousin.

Looking at the four of them, my heart swells and two thoughts collide: *Life hasn't always turned out like I had planned,* and *It's a beautiful, abundant life.*

Today, I'm nearly two thousand miles from where I lived as a child, two thousand miles from a time and place where I first longed to be in control. And I'm infinitely farther emotionally and spiritually as I continually let go.

Let go of the illusion of control, and the desire to control.

Let go of anxious what-ifs for the future.

Let go of painful remember-whens of the past.

Let go of expectations and demands.

Let go of lies of the devil, and hold-me-back fears, and comparisons to others, and papier mâché coping mechanisms and limiting beliefs and *wanting to be anyone else but who God created me to be.*

I let go, and I harness myself to Jesus, the trustworthy One.

And I do so with the quiet assurance that I will continue to free-fall into abundance.

About the Author

The most extraordinary thing about Marie is how ordinary she is. Or perhaps it is her ability to lose things like grocery lists, phone numbers, and her car in the parking lot. When she isn't searching for lost things, she writes silly plays with her grandchildren, hangs out with her six adult children, reads, and hikes with Scott, her husband of thirty-five years. And always she seeks to shine light on the glorious, abundant life that is found in Christ.

Marie and Scott currently reside in Aurora, Colorado in a house that is always bursting at the seams with family and friends.

When she can find her laptop, she blogs at: https://into-abundance.com/.

Marie is a CDE certified Braillist but left her job with Aurora Public Schools to pursue her passion of empowering women through Christian life coaching. She is a certified life coach for women. You can learn more about this and request a free introductory session at https://into-abundance.com/into-abundance-life-coaching/.

To contact Marie for speaking opportunities, or just to connect, you can e-mail her at: IntoAbundanceCoaching@gmail.com.

CPSIA information can be obtained
at www.ICGtesting.com
Printed in the USA
BVHW041946121122
651818BV00018B/121

9 781955 043809